MW00951585

How To Use Your God Power

To Get Everything You Ever Wanted
and Live The Life of Your Dreams...

"The Master's Course"

Book 1

Richard Lee McKim Jr.

Copyright © 2013 Richard Lee McKim Jr.

All rights reserved.

ISBN: 1483978850

ISBN-13: 978-1483978857

DEDICATION:

This Book is Dedicated to My Brother

Bob McKim

Who Inspired Me When I Needed It,

Who Advised Me When I Needed It, and

Who Supported Me When I Needed It.

Thank You & I Love You!

These Are The 12 Audio CDs That Accompany Book 1 L921

It is important that you listen to the Audio Book as part of your study of this material. The Audio Book Contains Information, Descriptions, Explanations and the Complete Answers to the Chapter Quiz Questions. It has nearly 50% more material than the printed part of the book. Importantly, these Audio CDs include the complete Review of Book 1.

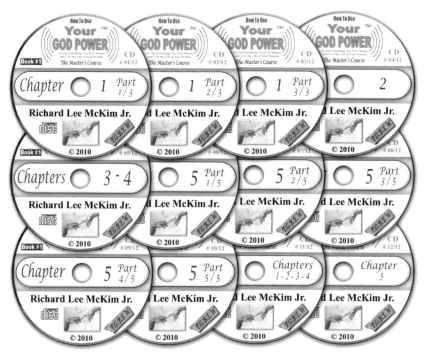

This CD set is Available in two formats: Electronic MP3 Download and Burned on actual CDs that can be played in any personal CD player, car CD player and on most Computers. The Electronic Download is included with your Purchase and is Free for you to download. **(Both Links Here)**

Free MP3 (12 CD) Download Included With Book Purchase: X659

Get The 12 CDs/Binder Set Delivered by the Postal Service: L923

Table Of Contents

How To Help Others From This Book
Using The "Ultra-Shareability" Features

It's Human nature to want to Help Your Family, Friends and Others, by sharing Great Ideas, Important Information, and Valuable Insights.

Today, the opportunity to share Your Insights, Thoughts, and Suggestions with Your Family, Friends and the World, is greater than ever with the Social Sharing Options that are now available, such as Twitter, FaceBook, Stumbled Upon, Linked-In and by E-Mail. These Social Platforms are the NEW way that *Word of Mouth* Recommendations, Opinions and Comments are Shared with Others and the World.

"Social Sharing is the Way We Help Each Other!"

This Book has been designed with *"Ultra-Shareability."* This Means that you can Quickly and Easily send Helpful and Useful Information to Anyone in the World right from this Book, by the Click of Your Mouse.

Every segment of this Book has Share Links Built in so that You can *Instantly Share* that Useful and Helpful Information with People You know by using the E-Mail Share Link, and/or share it with the entire World through the Social Media Platforms such as Twitter.

Never Has there been a better time to spread the word and share Your Enlightenment with the ones You Love and those who need it, and never has it been so quick and easy to do so.

 **Share This**

If Something "Resonates" With You,

You Should Use The Share Links Right Away,

Because You Know It's worth Sharing!

Sometimes the Help and Enlightenment that someone needs can only come from the thoughtfulness of another. Maybe something that You choose to Share with Someone Else may be the difference between Success or Failure, Happiness or Despair.

Throughout the Book, you will find four digit "Link Codes" in Blue which link to Course Videos, Audio Descriptions and Explanations, Photos & Illustrations, Video Examples, and References & additional Resources. They all start with one of these 5 Letters and are followed by 3 numbers.

C = Indicates Course Video Link
A = Audio Description/Explanation Link
V = Access Current Video Example Links
P = View/Download Course Photos/Illustrations
L = Direct Link to Course References/Resources

Here is the URL Link Formula:

www.TinyURL.com/GPB-C000 e or t

First Part of URL Link + 4 Digit Link Code + Extension

Here is an example of a **Course Video** Link:

 **www.TinyURL.com/GPB-C552**
The Course Video Links Will Open Up and Play The YouTube Course Video which Covers The Topic and Information You are reading. This Gives You the opportunity To Watch and/or listen to The corresponding Video as You read.

Here is an example of a Course **Audio Explanation** Link:

 www.TinyURL.com/GPB-A107
The Illustration Audio Descriptions, Explanations, and Quiz Answers are explained in great detail _**ONLY on the Videos and Audios**_. **When You See The Play Audio Link, (Starts with an "A") It is Highly Recommended That You use it to listen to the Audio Descriptions and Explanations that go with the Course.** When You Use The Audio Description /Explanation Link, You will Automatically Jump to the exact place in the Course Videos, where That Illustration Description and/or question is being Answered and Explained in great detail. Some of the descriptions and explanations are so in depth, that it requires several Audio Tracks or Videos Segments and You will see several Audio Links together.

Here is an example of a **Photos/Illustrations** Link:

www.TinyURL.com/GPB-P063

This PhotoBucket Link Will Automatically Open Up and Display Online Course Illustrations. You can then copy The Image from The PhotoBucket Website, to display on Your desktop, Send To Others, Post on Your Own Website or even Print It Out to hang it on your wall as a Poster. All of the Online Course Illustrations are **Free** To Download and Share With Anyone You Want.

Here is an example of a Course **Video Example** Link:

www.TinyURL.com/GPB-V224

The Video Example Links Will Open Up and Play The YouTube Course Video at the exact place where the Video Example is being explained. From there you will be able to click on and watch the Video Example. If the Video Example is not on YouTube, the Video Example Links will be in the Notes Section below the Course Video.

Here is an example of a **Reference/Resource** Link:

www.TinyURL.com/GPB-L512

This **Reference/Resource** Link Will Automatically Open Up the Web Page for that Reference and/or Resource for additional Information, study and follow up.

The Link Code Extensions "e" and "t"

Each of these Example Links will take you directly to the Course Videos, Photo/Illustrations, or Web Sites for that Link. However, this Book has special Sharing Features Built into the Link System. The sharing features are activated by adding an "e" or a "t" to the end of the Link. We can use this Course Video Link mentioned earlier:

www.TinyURL.com/GPB-C552

For Example: When this URL link is used as you see it, without any extensions, it will go directly to the Course Video and start playing the Video in the Exact same place that you are reading. *However....*

If you add an "**e**" to the end of the URL like this:

www.TinyURL.com/GPB-C552e

It will now Automatically open Your E-Mail Program and Insert The Link For The Corresponding Video *(At the Exact START Time)* or Illustration including the Subject Title. All You have To Do Is Insert One or More Email Addresses where you want the E-Mail to be sent and hit send! That Means that while you are reading the Book, if You think of Someone who would Benefit from the Information You are reading, you can immediately use the Link with the E-Mail "e" extension to send them the On-Line Link To the Video or Illustration so they can see it as well. Not only will they be thanking You for your thoughtfulness, But, You will really be helping them in a VERY REAL way.

The "e" Email extension can be added to <u>all the links</u> in this Book. You can turn a Course Video Link, Audio Explanation Link, Video Example Link, Picture/illustration Link or a Reference/Resource Link into an Email ready to send to anyone you want.

If you add a "**t**" to the end of the URL like this:

www.TinyURL.com/GPB-C552t

This Link Will now Automatically Connect to Your Twitter account and Post The Corresponding YouTube Video Link, PhotoBucket Illustration Link, or Reference Link, Including The Subject Title of the Link. You can immediately share the Illustrations, Course Videos, and Reference Links that are important to You.

The "t" Twitter extension can be added to <u>all the links</u> in this Book. You can turn a Course Video Link, Audio Explanation Link, Video Example Link, Picture/illustration Link or a Reference/Resource Link into a Twitter Posting (Tweet) to share with Your Followers and the World.

* Note: Capitalization does not matter. The same URL code above could be all caps: WWW.TINYURL.COM/GPB-C552T or written in all lower case: www.tinyurl.com/gpb-c552t Both work the same.

How (Why) I Created This Course

When I was looking for more Understanding on the Law of Attraction and Secrets of the Universe, I found that most of the Books available were mostly theory and vague Concepts or just outright "Fluff." Nothing was spelled out. My favorite Author/Guru Abraham-Hicks, always says "Ask and it is Given." This was seemingly easy enough, But, I wanted a Million Dollars, asked for it, and it still didn't show up? What about Great Relationships, Wonderful Health, Vibrant Love Life, and a Happy Joyful Life? I know that there are Millions of People like me who are asking for these things as well, and like me didn't get them. Why wasn't the "Law of Attraction" Working?

I KNOW that it is paramount to Believe in Your Ability and the Abundance of the Universe if the Law of Attraction is going to work for you. BUT, none of these Gurus, or their Books explained EXACTLY how these Universal Laws really work and how to use them.

I knew that if I could find out EXACTLY how the "Attraction" part works (Step by Step) and how it is "Activated" (Step by Step) then my Belief would skyrocket, and if I had unshakable Belief (KNOWING) then I could attract Anything and Everything I ever wanted.

I wanted this Unshakable Belief in the Law of Attraction and the Abundance of the Universe. So, I started on my own personal

"Quest For KNOWING."

In my search for the TRUE Secrets of The Universe, I found that there were so many Experts, Gurus and Researchers who each had a separate "Piece" of the puzzle. I realized that if I could gather all of these Authors' Research, Discoveries, Understandings, and Concepts in one place, I would finally uncover the Secrets of the Universe, Reach absolute KNOWING and be able to Create my Dream Life.

When I started my Quest For KNOWING, I found Dr. Bruce Lipton who explained in a Video, that our cells respond to our Thoughts and that if we are stressed, our cells would automatically depress our immune system, or if we are Happy, Boost it to perfect health. Importantly, He proved that we have absolute control of our Bodies and that even our DNA can be changed by our thoughts. I then found DR. Ellen Langer, who discovered and Proved, with her research that Ageing can not only be stopped, but it can actually be reversed. I found Rupert Sheldrake who discovered that Dogs and Cats respond to our thoughts even if we are miles away. He even had Proof with His Video Taped Experiment. I found Cleve Baxter who demonstrated and proved that even Plants respond to our thoughts. I also found many other stories and examples of People doing amazing things from Seeing with their finger tips, to being able to Taste what was in someone else's mouth while they were under hypnosis.

All together I studied the amazing research and experimental findings from all of these Well Known Experts in their Fields including Bruce H. Lipton, PHD. Cell Biology, Dr. Wayne Dyer, Dr. Deepak Chopra, Michael Newton Past Life Regression, Dr. Ellen Langer, Psychologist at Harvard University., Rupert Sheldrake Researcher, Cleve Backster Polygraph Expert, Tony Robbins, Gregg Braden Author, Dr. Kenneth Ring Near Death Experiences, Amit Goswami, Ph.D, & John Hagelin, Ph. D. Theoretical Quantum Physicists, Dr. Charles Tart Out Of Body Experiences, Abraham-Hicks, Michael Talbot, Author of "The Holographic Universe," João Magueijo, Professor of Physics at Imperial College London, Professor Irving Kirsch, University of Connecticut, and Graham Hancock Author, just to name a few.

I wondered how were all of these amazing findings connected? How could this Knowledge be used to improve our Lives?

After about 4 Years of Research and more than 10,000 hours of study and writing, I was able to put together the research and findings from all of these amazing people into one complete understanding of the Universe and how it works. BUT, just understanding it, wasn't enough, I wanted to create a Step By Step Process so that anyone could Get Everything they ever wanted and live the life of their Dreams Quickly and Easily.

Mission Accomplished.

I called This Book "How To Use Your God Power" because it shows you how to change your Reality and Create Miracles like GOD does.

This Ability is Truly A "GOD Power"

C100   Introduction & Lesson #1

This Book came as quite a pleasant and unexpected, surprise. While researching the supernatural and other related and unexplainable phenomena, I discovered that there were patterns to these events, and that these patterns were evidence, that our "Reality" is not a static and innate aspect of Life as we have known it. Instead, Reality is a dynamic and ever changing aspect of personal experience. As it turns out, there is not one overall Reality that is consistent throughout the Universe, but instead, there are as many Realities as there are perceivers of Reality, and that they are all as personal and individual to each of us, as our own finger prints.

I will be presenting evidence in this book that cannot be explained in any other way. It is clear that we are actually more powerful and more capable, than we have ever known, to change our own Reality, and even change our whole World in ways that seem unbelievable, and yet, it is all true. Ironically, it is the unbelievable nature of our changeable Realities, that is the very reason that we don't fully and effectively exercise our amazing, GOD Power.

In this book, I will explain the mechanisms and functions of our Physical Reality, and how its design works so well to appear "Realistic" in every detail. But, however magnificent Physical Reality is, it does have what seem like "Flaws" in its design, which reveal its true nature. These apparent "Flaws" in the Reality Mechanism, have become evident due to man's evolving use of his magnificent GOD Power, and expanding belief in himself, which has outpaced Physical Reality's ability to maintain a "Realistic" Physical Experience. However disconcerting these flaws in Physical Reality's "Realism," the gaps in its "Realistic appearance" are justified and explained as "Supernatural Occurrences," which actually gives them validity.

It will become clear that Physical Reality, is merely an elaborate illusion, not too different from the Reality that was depicted in the movie, "The Matrix." However, our imaginary Reality is not created by machines or some super computer, but instead, by us, the participants, who are experiencing it firsthand. It is a marvelous creation, which offers us a way to experience a physical state of being that is far different from that which we could have experienced in our true "form" as nonphysical beings of pure positive energy.

I will teach you how to use your GOD Power in effective ways, to accomplish anything and everything that you have ever wanted to in your Life Experience. Nothing is outside your ability, when you are using your GOD Power. However, it does take discipline, and practice to use it well. But, mastery over your GOD Power, will directly equate to mastery over your own Reality and your Life.

This book is geared to KNOWING. Knowing is Belief on Steroids. Knowing is the basis of your Reality. If you can reach KNOWING, you have absolute and complete control of your life. To assist you in learning this material, I have included Video Examples. These Videos are a bonus, to your learning. While it is not necessary to view the Videos, because the information about them is complete in this book, it will add additional clarity and confidence to your KNOWING. Since, "Seeing is Believing," these Videos are a bonus learning opportunity for those who are eager to really understand this material, and want to learn more.

I have also included Chapter Review information. These are the "Cliffs Notes" of each chapter. It is the main points that you should KNOW. After the Chapter Review Notes, I have included a Chapter Quiz. This is designed to further clarify the material. The answers are in the back of the book. It is my intention to assist you in every way that I can, to reach KNOWING, and when you do, the World will belong to you.

It is important to read the entire book because, I have "Distributed" the main points that you need to know throughout the entire Book. Each of the most important points in this book could have been made again and again in every chapter. However, if I had made the main points in every place that they were appropriate, this book would have been at least three times as big as it already is. So, I have selected a certain group of main points for each Chapter including the chapter on "What is Theoretically Possible," which I think is the most interesting and thought provoking Chapter in the Book.

In writing this book, I unfolded it in a logical progression. However, as I mentioned above, so many points that I didn't get to until later in the book, are so fundamental and important to every Chapter, that I highly recommend that you read this book at least twice to get the most out of it. Once you have read it through the first time, the information and comprehensive understanding you will then have, will serve you well in your second reading. You will get so much more out of your second reading, once you understand the whole book.

Books Inform, Courses Teach!

This is not a Book, it's a "Course." As a course, it has many elements that when used together will facilitate the best learning experience. With this Course, You can:

Read the Material, Listen to the Material, **&** Watch the Material.

First, the Book itself has more than 500 pages full of Information, pictures and illustrations to help explain the material and important points. The Audio Tracks, (Audio-Book 35+ Hours) have at least two hundred more pages of information in "Audio Form" that are not covered in the book (13+ Hours More than the Book). Not only does the Audio Track have more information, but, it also powerfully conveys the information by how the material is read and explained. Additionally, the Audio Tracks have "Sound-Illustrations" and "Audio-Quotes" where I not only read the Important Quotes written in the book, but, I also include the Audio Clips of the actual people speaking their own Quotes.

This Course also includes more than 100 Video Examples which add a high degree of validity to the material and also help to make the important points that convey the material in a powerful way. You should make it a point to watch the Videos that accompany this material.

It includes "Animated Illustrations" & the Video Examples which help to powerfully make the important points of the Course. This is a very easy way to quickly cover and learn the material.

The Best way to cover this Material is to Read the Book first with the Audio Tracks Playing at the same time. When you come to a Video Example, pause the Audio, and Watch the Video, then continue. After you have completed the entire Book, then watch the Course Videos as your "Second Read."

The Video Examples are all included in the Slide Presentation as well, so that you can cover all the material in this format as well. It is not as important or necessary to View the Videos the Second time around because you should still remember them.

Enjoy...

Lesson #1

I am giving you Lesson #1 right at the start of this book, because, you will need to make a decision after the end of this lesson of whether or not you should continue reading this book. Your "Reality," is based on your awareness and beliefs. There is nothing about your Reality that can't be changed. Even the "Laws of physics," such as fire burns things, and gravity, are only "Laws" for those who believe in them.

Becoming aware of certain kinds of knowledge, will affect and change your Reality. This is like the story of the Tree of Knowledge, which bears "informational fruits." This book is just such a fruit. Once you read it, your perception and conception of your Reality will forever be changed in ways that may be impossible to undo.

This is where you must be particular as to what material and information you read, what movies and shows you watch, and what kind of people you interact with. You MUST choose your influences wisely.

If you read this book and watch the associated Video Examples, your concept of Reality will be stretched to the limit and forever changed. You will no longer be able to believe in "one Reality for all," or that physics and the physical processes of Life on Earth, are governed by "Laws" that are fixed and unchangeable. You will realize that every single thing that you thought was an absolute, is actually flexible and voluntary.

Like in the movie, "The Matrix," you must decide whether to continue reading this book now and face these new truths, or put it down, and remain in the comfort of your current Reality as it is. All I'm offering is the truth and a complete understanding of how Reality really is.

Let the Quest for KNOWING Begin...

P063   # The God Power Philosophy:

Basic & Foundational Concepts

#1) The Facts & Circumstances DO NOT CREATE REALITY. Meaning is What Creates & Elicits Reality. Meaning Creates Vibration Which Resonates With And Activates Everything That Is Like It in The Universe. You Have The Power To Decide on The Meaning to Create The Reality You Want.

#2) There is NO Right Answer in The Universe. It Doesn't Matter Whether You Go Left or You Go Right, As Long as You Decide That You Are Going The Best Way. Then The Way You Go BECOMES The Correct/Best Path By DECISION.

#3) You Are in The Perfect Place Right Now. From Where You Are, With What You Have, You Have The Ability to "Elicit" Whatever it Takes to Get to Where Ever You Want to Go. If You Go Left & You End Up on Top of a Mountain, You Will Elicit a Helicopter to Get to Where You Want to Go. If You Go Right And End Up on The Beach, You Will Elicit a Boat That Will Take You Where You Want to Go. If You Need Money, You Will Elicit a Way to Get it. It Doesn't Matter What Your Circumstances Are, What You Have, or Where You Are.

However, If At Any Point, You Think That Things Have Gone Wrong, Then You Will NOT Be Able to See The Solution Even Though It Is Lying At Your Feet. If This Happens, Go Back To #1.

"Let Your Quest For Knowing, Continue!"

Contact: YourGodPower@gmail.com

Important Notice:

This Book is full of examples of people healing themselves by the use of their God Power without any medical treatment. However, that requires total Faith and a complete understanding of how the Universe works. You will get both by reading this Book.

However, while it is possible for You to heal Yourself this way as well, You should consult with Your own Doctor before embarking on any new method of healing. You might even encourage Your Doctor to read this Book so that He/She is fully aware of Your plans.

Additionally, it is very important to understand that the normal accepted treatment by Medical Professionals may be the EXACT and BEST solution for Your current situation. As You will learn in this Book, it is not what You do, (Go to a Doctor or not) but instead, it is what You think about what You are doing. High confidence in Your Doctor could have better results than low confidence in any other alternative solutions.

This Means that by reading this Book, You could Improve the Results of Your current medical treatment without making any changes, just by having more Faith in Your own ability to be healed. Remember, You are in the Perfect Place right now, to get to where ever You want to go. *(See The God Power Philosophy)* It makes perfect sense to give Your current Medical Treatment and Doctor a chance to "BECOME" the perfect solution for You, as You "BECOME" the perfect patient.

Before making any drastic changes in Your Life, make the Changes in Yourself. You may find that once You have changed Yourself, Your Life will seem perfect as it is. Once You "BECOME" the *New You*, then the NEW YOU will automatically know what to do from where You are now.

To "BECOME" the New You, Read this Book several times until You feel the excitement of Living Your Life. Then Go For Your Dreams. They are ALL within Reach. Richard Lee McKim Jr.

Richard Lee McKim Jr.

Part I

YOUR GOD POWER & PURPOSE

C101

Richard Lee McKim Jr.

Notes - Thoughts - Insights

Chapter 1

Your GOD Power   C102

All great philosophies and religions say that we were made in GOD's image. What does that mean? What is an "Image" any way? Of course most of us think of an "Image" as a picture or how something looks. Obviously it's not how we look, because we all look different. But, then "Image" does mean "Likeness." It must be that we were made in the "Likeness" of GOD. But that raises a whole new bunch of questions. How are we like GOD? Is it because we think? Is it having thoughts? No, that can't be right either, because animals think and have thoughts too. So, what makes us "Like" GOD but different than animals? Is it because we make decisions? No, that's not it either. Animals decide if something is good to eat or whether they are in danger or not. So, what is the answer then? It has to be "Like" GOD on the one hand, but at the same time different than animals, but, it's not thinking, thoughts, or deciding. We must have a special "Ability or Power," "Like" GOD, that animals don't have. It must be a "GOD POWER." What is this special GOD Power? What is it and how does it work? This "GOD POWER" that we all have, must be something special if GOD has it too. It must be a very powerful and special gift for us, if we have it and animals don't. But what is this mysterious GOD Power that we all have and how can we start using it?

Your GOD Power is very simple and easy to use, and yet, it is the most powerful ability known to man.

> ## Your GOD Power Is The Ability To
> ## Change Reality, By Assigning Meaning

There is nothing else that even comes close to this GOD Power. This is the One Power that GOD has, and with it he created the Universe and everything in it. The entire Universe and everything in it, including us, are made up of, and created from, Pure Energy. The only Power and ability that is necessary to create the Universe from Energy is the ability to Define and assign Meaning to the Energy and it becomes.

What is a Planet and what is the Meaning of a Planet? It is the definition of, and the meaning of Earth that forms it and maintains it. There is definition and meaning in a Star, a Planet, and a Human Life. It is through assigning meaning that anything can be manifested from the energy of the Universe. Without meaning, there is nothing. Nothing can exist without already having definition and meaning. This includes everything from solid matter, to non physical things such as situations, circumstances and events. They all exist and have meaning. This is GOD's Power and because we were made in his "Image," we have it too.

Yes, you have the same Power as GOD, but, it is somewhat Muted in your Human experience because of "Immersion" which you will learn about later in this book. It is through your "Immersion" that you use your GOD Power to create and form the boundaries of your own Physical Human experience. More on that later...

So, how do you use your GOD Power and why is it so great? While you will get a better understanding of this as this book unfolds, I will give you a few examples of how it works right now, just to get you started. Many of you in the self help fields will recognize this information. Only now you will get a better understanding of how and why it works. I am speaking of "Visualization." It's not exactly "Visualization" that is the key, but, "Visualization" is one method of asserting Meaning. Before you can really understand Visualization, you first must understand how your Mind (Not your Brain) works.

I always get a good laugh whenever I hear someone say, "You are tricking the Brain, because it doesn't know whether you are actually performing the exercise or just imagining it." They say this because they really don't understand the "Reality Mechanism." Everything that you do is giving meaning. This is like animals. When you exercise, you are communicating, in a physical way "This activity is working these muscles and as a result will cause muscle growth." That IS the meaning of lifting weight. So, where ever there is meaning, (And there is always meaning) there is the result and response to that meaning. The muscle gets bigger and stronger. It is important to note, that the muscle is not responding to the exercise, but to the meaning of the exercise. Everything is operating on meaning, always on meaning, only on meaning and nothing but meaning. So when animals run, the meaning is "the muscle is exercising" and the result and response (to the meaning) is stronger muscle. So far we are just like animals, we do something, which has meaning, and then we get a result from that activity that had meaning.

Remember the result is always from the meaning and NOT from the activity itself. The activity itself, only serves to convey a certain MEANING. That is all it does.

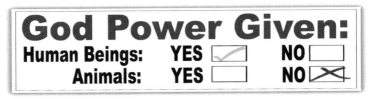

Here is where we use our GOD Power to accomplish things that animals have no way to match. (By the way, I use animals by comparison, because it is easy to see the difference between those who have GOD Power, Humans, and those who do not, animals.) We will be using exercise by lifting weights, as our example. While we are lifting the weight, in our mind, we can change the meaning of what we are doing. In our mind only, we can see ourselves as lifting a heavier weight, doing more exercise, than we are actually physically doing. The result? Of course, the muscles get even bigger than they would have been before, because the result/response is always based on the meaning and not the actual activity. In fact, there have been many studies that have shown that those who didn't even exercise at all (No physical movement at all), but only visualized the weight lifting activity in their minds, built exactly as much muscle as those who actually did the hard work and actually exercised. This is because, both of these groups were giving meaning to what they were doing, one by actually doing it, and the other just by visualizing it. Naturally, for an animal to get stronger, the only choice it has is to give the meaning by actually running, because it has no ability to assign or give meaning in any other way. You can begin to see how powerful and valuable this ability to create and assign meaning is.

Richard Lee McKim Jr.

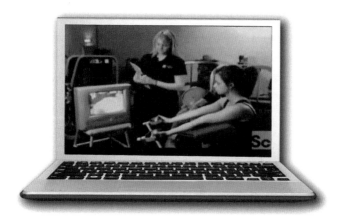

Video Example Exercising By Visualization
V103   Gets the Same Results [1]

What is this video about?

Visualizing exercise can and does work as well as actually exercising. In this Video Example, the researchers first test the natural ability of all the volunteers. Once they have the initial physical ability established, they divide the group in two. One group works out by actually lifting weights and doing some very strenuous exercise, while the other group simply thinks about lifting the weight in their mind.

In order to assist the visualization process, the researchers filmed these volunteers from behind as they were actually doing the exercise during the first testing stage. They then played the actual video of the participant, from the participants' point of view, while they were sitting at the exercise machine. So, everything was the same except that they didn't actually lift the weight, they only watched themselves doing it, and sat at the machine as if they were doing it. The results? After several weeks of "Training," the Visualizers amazingly, built more muscle than those who actually lifted the weights and did the hard training.

What does this example show and what does it mean?

What this Video Example shows is that it is the MEANING that is actually accomplishing anything. The actual Lifting only gives Meaning. That's it. When you lift heavy weight, you convey absolute and clear Meaning. However, when you visualize lifting, and get the feeling like you are really doing the lifting, you are also conveying meaning. Both are equally powerful.

This Video Example proves that we can easily substitute physically created Meaning for Mentally created Meaning. That is Your GOD Power, to assert Meaning, and create Meaning at will. And since our entire existence is a function of MEANING, if we can decide what that Meaning is, we have absolute control over our own Life Experience with our GOD Power.

Just so I'm clear about Physically generated Meaning and Thought generated Meaning, I want to stress that we came here for the physical experience; the fun and exhilaration of the physical action and feeling. So, using physical means to assert and create Meaning is perfectly fine, in fact it is preferred. It is just that when using your GOD Power, to adjust meanings, change Meanings or assert new Meanings, it is not always easy to assert the new meaning in a physical way. More often than not, it will have to be a mental thought process. But, by all means, enjoy your physical expressions and physical experience because that's what you're here for.

(1) Weird Connections is a fast-paced and entertaining glimpse at the strangest experiments being performed in the name of science today. On the surface these experiments seem so "out there" that it's hard to believe they're more than late-night lab pranks. researchers put a roach in the driver's seat of an electric powered vehicle; or use gravity-defying frogs to help mankind colonize Mars; or force locusts to watch Star Wars in order to help develop safer automobiles. Each episode takes the viewer on an unlikely and unexpected journey, plotting the connections between one amazing experiment and the next and ending with the real scientific advances they have inspired. **L104**

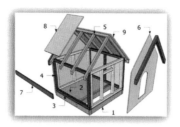

C105 The Many Levels of Meaning

Before we go any farther, we really need to understand the mechanics of Meaning. Meaning is present at every single layer and every single viewpoint and at every nook and cranny of every situation. Everything is built and created from Meaning.

Just to show you how pervasive Meaning is in our experience, I will build a simple doghouse built out of Meaning. First, the location has meaning. It is in a certain spot, that is within a certain area that is has the meaning of being owned by a certain person. It is built of wood that has a meaning that was created by the kind of tree that it came from. Its meaning dictates certain properties. You put wood on top, which has the meaning that when a certain substance called water which has a meaning and certain properties, the meaning of a roof keeps the meaning of the water from entering the space which has a meaning of what is enclosed by the wood. Furthermore the meaning of wood prevents the meaning of light from passing through it, where the meaning of glass, does allow the meaning of light to pass, but not the meaning of water.

You can quickly see that the Universe has the most powerful computational abilities you could ever imagine to keep track of all the assigned meanings and still make sure they are all interacting properly. All meaning is calculated and reconciled at the energy level and then only "Represented" at the physical level. (We will go into great detail about "Representations, later in this book.) While the energy level can be best described as in another dimension, we can visualize it better if we think of it as a cloud above every person, object and situation. This would be like a higher level of activity or consciousness. Let's look at a Meaning diagram for the exercise example above.

Normal Workout			A106
Physical Meaning of Person	+ Physical Meaning of weight	+ Physical Meaning of lifting	= Physical Meaning Result (More muscle)

GOD Power (Exercised By Visualization)			A107 P020
Physical Meaning of Person	+ Thought Meaning of weight	+ Thought Meaning of lifting	= Physical Meaning Result (More muscle)

Building Muscle Meanings Have Been Activated & Are Being Elicited From The Situation

The Green Tuning Fork Vibrations are Positive Meanings and they Resonate & Elicit ALL the things that will make them Stronger. Notice that the THOUGHT of working out elicits all the SAME muscle building activities that actually working out does

The Red Tuning Fork Vibrations are Negative Meanings and they Resonate & Elicit ALL the things that will make them weaker. Notice that the RED Tuning forks are not "Activated in this example and as a result they do not respond and cause no Harm

At this point, I need to explain the Green and Red "Tuning Forks" illustration above. Throughout this book, these tuning forks will give you a visual image of how the Meaning Process is working and activating appropriate responses. In this example, you have the Meaning of Exercise which could be represented by the "Green Tuning Forks." When a certain Meaning is initiated, it elicits from the situation all those things that are "like it" and brings them into action. At the same time, all those responses that are not relevant to the Meaning asserted, like the red Tuning Forks, do not respond and are not activated. The meaning of exercising causes all the responses needed to create Muscle to become activated. Some call this the "Law of Attraction," where like attracts like. Once you read the section on "Frequencies and Resonance" you will really understand the Meanings that these Tuning Forks represent.

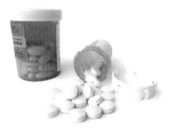

C108   Example #2

We just saw an example of using GOD Power to improve muscle building, now, in this example, we will see a medical application. You have been told that you have a serious Life threatening disease. You are given a special medicine that will cure you. You take it and you are cured. What happened here? I know what you are thinking, and no, I'm not going to tell you about the Placebo... not yet. This was real medicine and it really cured a serious sickness. I am using this rather "Normal" example, so that I can explain just how the "Meaning Mechanism" works. First, there was actually a disease present. It had a meaning generated by its chemical and physical properties. Next, the miracle drug has a meaning derived and generated by its chemical content. Then, the combination and interaction between the meaning of the disease and the meaning of the medicine resulted in a cure in the same way as 2 + 2 = 4. It's a very simple equation. When an animal has a disease and you give it the right medicine to cure it, the same result is had. The meaning of the disease interacts with the meaning of the medicine given, and the resulting cure is had. Once again, the meanings were derived from the meanings already present in the animal and the chemical makeup of the medicine.

Normal Reality				A109
Physical +	Physical +	Physical +	Physical =	Physical
Meaning	Meaning	Meaning	Meaning	Meaning
of Person	of Disease	Pill In	Real Medicine	Result:
		Mouth		CURE

It is important to understand that in our Universe, there is meaning already present. That's what animals go by, the meaning already present and assigned. Our GOD Power is the ability to assign Meaning and/or change the meaning that is already present as we choose.

Example #3   C110

As before, you have been told that you have a serious life threatening disease. However, the doctor doesn't have a cure for this one. So he gives you a "Sugar Pill" which is called a "Placebo." This is FAKE medicine. The chemical makeup of this pill has the meaning of a tic tack or candy. However, he tells you that it is a miracle drug that will easily cure your illness. So you take it, and just as expected, the disease is cured. So, what happened here?

First, you had the meaning of the disease generated by the chemical makeup and properties that it possessed, and then you had the meaning of the pill. But, here is the special part. You assigned a new meaning to this pill that it was now a "Trump Card." That no matter how powerful this disease, this would match it and result in a "win" over this disease, a cure. So, the meaning of the disease is combined with the meaning of the medicine, which is now a trump card (Beats all Miracle Cure), which automatically wins by definition & meaning, and you get a result of a cure.

Normal Reality					A111
Physical Meaning of Person	+ Physical Meaning of Disease	+ Physical Meaning Pill In Mouth	+ Physical Meaning Medicine (Sugar)	=	Physical Meaning Result: **No CURE**

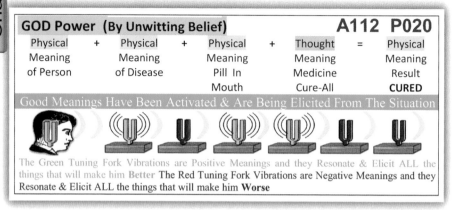

GOD Power (By Unwitting Belief)				A112 P020
Physical +	Physical +	Physical +	Thought =	Physical
Meaning	Meaning	Meaning	Meaning	Meaning
of Person	of Disease	Pill In	Medicine	Result
		Mouth	Cure-All	**CURED**

Good Meanings Have Been Activated & Are Being Elicited From The Situation

The Green Tuning Fork Vibrations are Positive Meanings and they Resonate & Elicit ALL the things that will make him **Better** The Red Tuning Fork Vibrations are Negative Meanings and they Resonate & Elicit ALL the things that will make him **Worse**

This is where we differ from animals. You can't give an animal a sugar pill, because the only thing that would happen is you would give the animal a sugar rush. You combine the meaning of the disease the animal has, generated by the chemical and physical properties of the disease, with the meaning of the pill generated by its chemical and physical properties, which is actually sugar, and you will get the expected result – NO CURE.

If they would have given you the fake sugar pill while you were asleep, or in a coma, it would not have been effective either, because for it to work, YOU had to assign meaning to it and you can only do that consciously. If you had received it unconsciously, the meaning would have remained that of a sugar pill.

Yes you were tricked into using your GOD Power to assign a different meaning to the sugar pill. In this case it worked out great for you. But, the thing is, we are all using our GOD Power all the time. We are always assigning meaning to everything that happens and to everything we think about and do. Many people have died when they didn't have to, because they used their GOD Power poorly.

Example #4   C113

A person has just been told that they have a serious life threatening disease. In their panic, they call their best friend to tell them the bad news. The friend says "That's too bad. I have heard that, what you have is a terminal situation and that nobody has ever survived that disease." He feels really bad now and it all seems hopeless. The Doctor comes in and says "We have an experimental drug that might work for you. Would you like to try it?" He agrees because something is better than nothing. The Doctor gives him the new drug. The patient dies anyway. What happened here?

First, there was the meaning of the disease generated by the chemical and physical properties of the disease, and then there was the meaning of the medicine based on the chemical and physical properties of the drug. In this case the meaning of the drug was that it really was a miracle drug that was able to cure the meaning of the disease. However, the patient assigned a different meaning to the disease that it was so powerful, that it could not be defeated. The disease became a trump card that prevented any other meaning from curing the disease, and it prevented a drug that would have otherwise cured him, from working.

Normal Reality					A114
Physical Meaning of Person	+ Physical Meaning of Disease	+ Physical Meaning Pill In Mouth	+ Physical Meaning Medicine Is Real	=	Physical Meaning Result: **CURED**

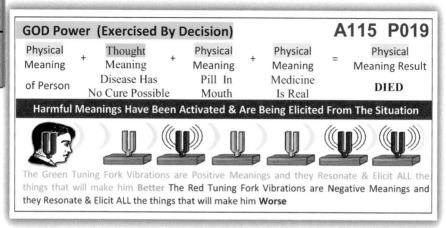

GOD Power (Exercised By Decision)				A115 P019
Physical Meaning of Person	+ Thought Meaning Disease Has No Cure Possible	+ Physical Meaning Pill In Mouth	+ Physical Meaning Medicine Is Real	= Physical Meaning Result **DIED**

Harmful Meanings Have Been Activated & Are Being Elicited From The Situation

The Green Tuning Fork Vibrations are Positive Meanings and they Resonate & Elicit ALL the things that will make him **Better** The Red Tuning Fork Vibrations are Negative Meanings and they Resonate & Elicit ALL the things that will make him **Worse**

C116   Two Real Life Case Studies

Real Case #1

In this next Video Example, we will see a case where a man died because he thought that he was supposed to. He was convinced that he had an incurable disease and so he asserted the Meaning that he would die and he did. Later it turned out that the disease had been cured by the operation, if only he had known.

V117   Video Example - Man Dies from Placebo Effect

What is this video about?

This video is about a case in 1974. Sam Londe, a retired shoe salesman had cancer of the esophagus, which is the tube running from the mouth to the stomach. Even though the doctors had surgically removed all the cancer they could find, they were sure that it would return. In 1974, this kind of cancer was KNOWN to be 100% fatal and there was no chance that Sam would survive. Sam died a few weeks later which was no surprise to anyone. However, after the autopsy, it was discovered that even though they did find a small amount of cancer, it wasn't in the esophagus, and clearly it wasn't the cause of his death. He could have easily survived the cancer that he had. He died because he thought he was supposed to. He believed that he was going to die and he did. The Cancer that they found was so tiny and nobody even knew that it was there. Everyone thought he was going to die from his throat cancer, and so they thought that he did.

What does this example show and what does it mean?

The importance of this Video Example is that Meanings can save you or they can kill you. So, what happened in this situation? First there was the meaning of the Cancer in his esophagus, which was nothing. There wasn't any there. As it turned out, it had all been successfully removed. So there was no Disease Meaning present in his throat.

However, then you add in the "Meaning" of the situation asserted by the Doctors and felt by Sam, that he was going to die for sure from this cancer. So the Meaning he asserted of "I'm going to die," was more powerful than the actual meaning that he had no cancer in his throat any more, and so he died. The Meaning of imminent death, "elicited" a death response from his body. **Note:** When asserting Meanings with your GOD Power, be sure to always go for the Better Meaning.

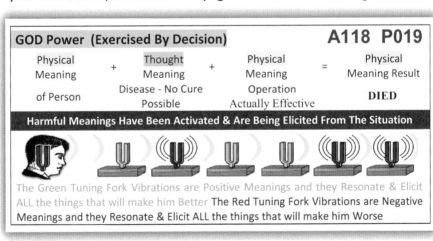

In these prior examples, we changed the meaning of a pill that we actually ingested or an operation that we actually had. However, we are not limited to changing the meaning of physical matter; we can change and assign meaning to events, circumstances and situations that have no physical form.

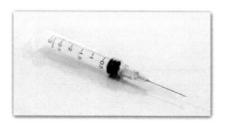

C119   **Real Case #2**

So far we have seen Examples where someone has lived because of the Placebo effect or they have died because of it. Now we will see a case where the same man first had a Miracle Recovery from Cancer and lived because of the Placebo Effect and then later had a catastrophic relapse of Cancer and died because of the Placebo Effect. Your Beliefs and Meanings are the Source of Life or Death. What something Means to you and you Believe to be True, Becomes True, for you. That is the Placebo Effect, for the Good or the Bad.

No incident better illustrates this than a now famous case reported by psychologist Bruno Klopfer. [2] Klopfer was treating a man named Wright[3] who had advanced cancer of the lymph nodes. All standard treatments had been exhausted, and Wright appeared to have little time left. His neck, armpits, chest, abdomen, and groin were filled with tumors the size of oranges, and his spleen and liver were so enlarged that two quarts of milky fluid had to be drained out of his chest every day.

But Wright did not want to die. He had heard about an exciting new drug called Krebiozen, and he begged his doctor to let him try it. At first his doctor refused because the drug was only being tried on people with a life expectancy of at least three months. But Wright was so unrelenting in his entreaties, his doctor finally gave in.

He gave Wright an injection of Krebiozen on Friday, but in his heart of hearts he did not expect Wright to last the weekend. Then the doctor went home.

To his surprise, on the following Monday he found Wright out of bed and walking around. Klopfer reported that his tumors had "melted like snowballs on a hot stove" and were half their original size.

This was a far more rapid decrease in size than even the strongest X-ray treatments could have accomplished. Ten days after Wright's first Krebiozen treatment, he left the hospital and was, as far as his doctors could tell, Cancer Free. When he had entered the hospital he had needed an oxygen mask to breathe, but when he left he was well enough to fly his own plane at 12,000 feet with no discomfort.

Wright remained well for about two months, but then articles began to appear asserting that Krebiozen actually had no effect on cancer of the lymph nodes. Wright, who was rigidly logical and scientific in his thinking, became very depressed, suffered a relapse, and was readmitted to the hospital. This time his physician decided to try an experiment.

He told Wright that Krebiozen was every bit as effective as it had seemed, but that some of the initial supplies of the drug had deteriorated during shipping. He explained, however, that he had a new highly concentrated version of the drug and could treat Wright with this.

Of course the physician did not have a new version of the drug and intended to inject Wright with plain water. To create the proper atmosphere he even went through an elaborate procedure before injecting Wright with the placebo.

Again the results were dramatic. Tumor masses melted, chest fluid vanished, and Wright was quickly back on his feet and feeling great.

---

(2) Bruno Klopfer (1900-1971) He was born in Bavaria, Germany on 1 October, 1900. He had a profound impact on the development of psychological personality testing, and was an important pioneer and innovator in the development, scoring and popularization of projective techniques especially the Rorschach inkblot test. **L123**

(3) Klopfer, B., "Psychological Variables in Human Cancer", Journal of Projective Techniques, Vol.21, No.4, (December 1957), pp.331-340. (This paper is also significant because it contains an account of the impact of the treatment of a Lymphosarcoma upon Mr. Wright, a patient of one of Klopfer's colleagues (Dr. Philip West) with a bogus medicine, "Krebiozen'". Klopfer's account of Wright's progress is often referred to in the cancer literature, but the actual reference is seldom cited.) **L124**

Normal Reality

Physical Meaning of Person	+	Physical Meaning of Disease	+	Physical Meaning Injected With Water	+	Physical Meaning Medicine (Just Water)	=	Physical Meaning Result Patient **Dies**

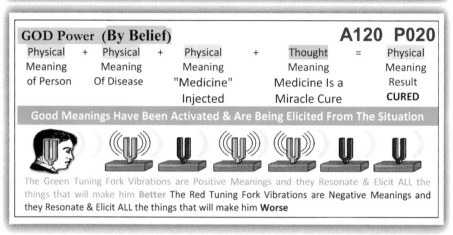

GOD Power (By Belief)   **A120 P020**

Physical Meaning of Person	+	Physical Meaning Of Disease	+	Physical Meaning "Medicine" Injected	+	Thought Meaning Medicine Is a Miracle Cure	=	Physical Meaning Result **CURED**

Good Meanings Have Been Activated & Are Being Elicited From The Situation

The Green Tuning Fork Vibrations are Positive Meanings and they Resonate & Elicit ALL the things that will make him **Better** The Red Tuning Fork Vibrations are Negative Meanings and they Resonate & Elicit ALL the things that will make him **Worse**

He remained symptom-free for another two months, but then the American Medical Association announced that a nationwide study of Krebiozen had found the drug worthless in the treatment of cancer. This time Wright's faith was completely shattered.

His cancer Showed Up again and he died two days later. [45]

There are several Important Points to get from this Case. First, Wright, the patient, really believed in the new Drug Krebiozen. Also, since the Drug was hard to get and he even had to beg his Doctor to get it, it seemed even more "Valuable" and "REAL."

Even though he was at Deaths' Door, with tumors the size of Oranges and two quarts of milky fluid being extracted from his chest every day, and even his Doctor expected him to die within a day or two, he still believed that he could be cured if only he could get this new "Miracle Drug."

---

(4) Bruno Klopfer, "Psychological Variables in Human Cancer," Journal of Prospective Techniques 31 (1957),pp. 331-40.

(5) Story Retold By Michael Talbot in his book "The Holographic Universe" Harper Perennial, 1991, Page 94.

So from that place of extreme Belief and Faith in the new Drug, Krebiozen, he had a Miraculous Recovery. His Cancer Tumors had "melted like snowballs on a hot stove." He left the Hospital "Cancer-Free." He had completely Healed. Since the Drug was later found to be useless, we Know that he "Cured Himself" solely on the Basis of his Belief and Faith in the Drug and not because it was actually effective.

This situation could be compared to our Sugar Pill Example we saw earlier. The Actual Chemical Properties and Makeup of the Drug had a Meaning of "No Cure", just like the Sugar Pill did, and just like the prior Example, he assigned a Meaning to it of a "Miracle Cure." So the Meaning that he gave it with his GOD Power "Became" the Drug's REAL MEANING. He MADE IT A MIRACLE CURE by thinking that it was. So he lived.

Importantly, even though the "Drug" was long gone out of his system, it's Meaning was still powerfully keeping him well and Cancer Free. The Meaning Remained "In his system."

Later, rather than just accepting his cure and living the rest of his life Cancer Free, he continued to Worry about his situation. His life was "Tied to the Meaning of that Drug." So as the Meaning of the Drug changed so did his life.

At first, he had given the Drug his own Meaning of a Miracle Cure and it "Became" exactly what he thought it was. But then, he keep reading about the Drug, and what other people thought about it, and then he changed his own Meaning of the Drug to match the Meaning that the "Others" had given it.

This is why you MUST be very careful when listening to the opinions of others. When you accept their opinions, you accept their MEANINGS, Good or Bad.

This now changed everything. "If that Drug wasn't REALLY a Miracle Cure, then he must not have REALLY been Cured." Therefore he MUST still have Cancer, and so he then Created it for himself. In the same way that he created a Miracle Drug by his Meanings, he created Cancer. Both were powerfully effective. One created a Miracle Recovery in ten days, and the other Created a Catastrophic Relapse that Killed him in two days.

Chapter 1

So, at first there was no REAL Drug to cure him but he created a Miracle Drug from nothing by his thoughts, his God Power, and then later there was no Cancer, but he created it from his thoughts by his GOD Power.

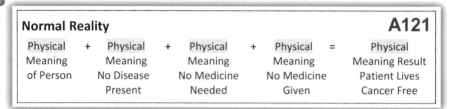

Normal Reality				A121
Physical +	Physical +	Physical +	Physical =	Physical
Meaning	Meaning	Meaning	Meaning	Meaning Result
of Person	No Disease	No Medicine	No Medicine	Patient Lives
	Present	Needed	Given	Cancer Free

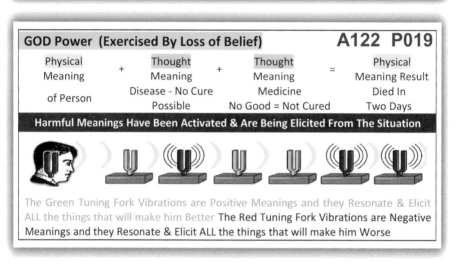

GOD Power (Exercised By Loss of Belief)			A122 P019
Physical +	Thought +	Thought =	Physical
Meaning	Meaning	Meaning	Meaning Result
of Person	Disease - No Cure	Medicine	Died In
	Possible	No Good = Not Cured	Two Days

Harmful Meanings Have Been Activated & Are Being Elicited From The Situation

The Green Tuning Fork Vibrations are Positive Meanings and they Resonate & Elicit ALL the things that will make him Better **The Red Tuning Fork Vibrations are Negative Meanings and they Resonate & Elicit ALL the things that will make him Worse**

C125   Example #5

As before, you have been told that you have a serious life threatening disease. This is quite a shock to you and you ask for a sleeping pill to get some needed rest. When you wake up, the nurse tells you that the Doctor has some good news for you. Excitedly, you await the Doctor. He comes in and tells you that while you were asleep, he had received some very special medicine and he has already given it to you through your I.V., while you were still asleep, and that the preliminary results look very promising. You heal as expected. However, what you didn't know is that the Doctor not only didn't have any special medicine, but he didn't even administer anything into your system. So what happened here?

First, you had the meaning generated by the chemical and physical properties of the disease, then you combine that with the meaning of a miracle drug already in your system and working, and the resulting meaning is that the disease goes away and is cured. Remember, it was not the meaning of the chemical properties of the sugar pill that cured the disease before, it was the meaning assigned by you. So, in effect, the actual meaning of the sugar pill, and even the actual physical pill itself was of no use. It was only useful to convey the meaning that you were "Taking Medicine" and the meaning that "It was now in your system." That was the only use the actual sugar pill gave you. But in this case, that wasn't even necessary because, you were told that it was already in your system. Therefore, you didn't need to see it "Go in," to believe it. The Doctor and nurse, after all, were credible people, and if they said they gave you the medicine, it must have happen.

Normal Reality

Physical	+	Physical	+	Physical	+	Physical	=	Physical
Meaning		Meaning		Meaning		Meaning		Meaning
of Person		Disease		Nothing Put		No Medicine		Result
				In Your System		At All		**NO CURE**

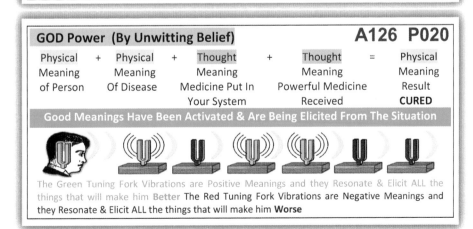

GOD Power (By Unwitting Belief)   **A126 P020**

Physical	+	Physical	+	Thought	+	Thought	=	Physical
Meaning		Meaning		Meaning		Meaning		Meaning
of Person		Of Disease		Medicine Put In		Powerful Medicine		Result
				Your System		Received		**CURED**

Good Meanings Have Been Activated & Are Being Elicited From The Situation

The Green Tuning Fork Vibrations are Positive Meanings and they Resonate & Elicit ALL the things that will make him **Better** The Red Tuning Fork Vibrations are Negative Meanings and they Resonate & Elicit ALL the things that will make him **Worse**

This kind of cure would never work for an animal, because if you didn't actually give them the medicine, there will be no cure. They go by the actual meaning of the chemical and physical properties of the medicine. This brings up another important aspect of your GOD Power, Belief. You must believe your own assigned meanings. If you didn't believe that the sugar pill was real medicine, it never could have worked. That's why, trickery works so well with placebos. If you were told that you were given a sugar pill, it would have continued to have the meaning of a sugar pill, and it never could have cured you.

Is there any limit to your ability to use your GOD Power to assign meaning? No, there isn't. While you have no actual limits on assigning meaning, you must believe those meanings that you have assigned, for them to work. Second, you only have the ability to assign meaning as it pertains to you. You cannot assign meaning to others without their belief in them.

You could find a nice size rock and say "That it is now gold." But unless you believed it, it wouldn't transform. If you believed in your ability enough, you could turn water into wine and rocks into bread. It is just a matter of changing the meaning of the energy that comprises the object.

So what are some practical uses of your GOD Power? You could think and declare that everything is working out for you. By giving your life experience the meaning that it's all working out for you, you could cause the meaning of any actual situation, to interact with the new meaning that it's working out for you, causing the situation to evolve into a good one for you. Where people might have said no, they will now say yes instead. This is why people have been talking about "positive thinking" all these years and getting great results. They have always known that it works, but not exactly why or how. It is because you have assigned the overall meaning to experiences involving you, that they will "Work Out." And like the sugar pill, this meaning that you have asserted interacts with the actual meaning generated from the elements of the circumstance, and results in a meaning that "Works out for you." How great is that?

That's why, when you know that things are working out for you, they are. Because if you KNOW that they are, that is stronger than belief, and it is as strong on your life circumstances, as the belief in the Placebo was on the actual disease that you had. Your assigned meaning is more powerful than ANY circumstantial meaning that is already present. Remember, your meaning, that you assigned with your GOD Power, can and will TRUMP any situation, if you believe in it.

In this next Video Example, we will see how the "Unwitting Belief" of a Doctor, resulted in a Miracle cure that would never had occurred otherwise.

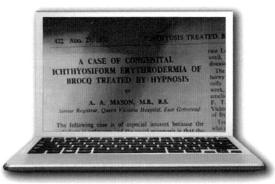

V127

Video Example The Case of the "Alligator Skinned" Boy

What is this video about?

In 1952, Albert Mason was an anesthesia specialist, at the Queen Victoria Hospital in East Grinstead, West Sussex, England. A patient was wheeled in to be put under, who looked like he had "Millions of Warts" covering his arms, legs and feet. Mr. Moor, the Surgeon on the case, had been unsuccessfully trying to graft skin from the 15 year old boy's chest, where there weren't any "Warts," to his hands. The Surgeon was quite displeased with the results that he was having.

Mason, who remarked that he was rather "Young and Cocky" at the time, said to the Surgeon, "Why don't you treat him with hypnotism?" The Surgeon replied, "Why don't you?" and walked out of the room. Mason had used hypnosis on several occasions with great success to remove warts, and so the next day he hypnotized the Boy.

While the boy was hypnotized, he gave the suggestion to the boy, "The Warts will fall off your right arm and new skin will grow there that is soft and normal." A week later the Boy returned with startling results. (The Pictures in the video are dramatic). The skin on the Boy's arm went from a disgusting blackened and scabby mess, to a normal bright colored skin like you would expect to see on any normal arm.

They went to show the Surgeon, Mr. Moore, but he was in surgery at the time. So, instead they stood outside the plate glass window, and he held up the boy's two arms for the Surgeon to see. The Surgeon's eyes were as big as saucers. He came right out to see the results for himself. He had a closer look and said "Good God!" Mason replied, "I told you that warts go." The Surgeon replied, "This isn't warts, this is a rare congenital disease that he was born with. It's incurable!"

What Albert Mason had done was considered IMPOSSIBLE. This disease normally claimed its victims in early childhood. But, this boy lived and is an old man today, living a normal life. After the news of his amazing success got out, he was inundated by requests of others who had the same disease, but he was unable to help any of them. None of them had responded like the young boy had.

However, there is an explanation. In Albert Mason's own words, "I now knew it was incurable. Beforehand, I thought that it was warts, and I had a conviction, that I can cure warts." His next words are the most powerful of all. He continues, "After that first case, I was acting. I knew it had no right to get well. Any you know, I'm sure that, that was conveyed."

What does this example show and what does it mean?

This is a powerful example of how Meanings are influenced and changed. This was a fortuitous set of circumstances that led to this boy's recovery. If any one thing had been different it would not have occurred. Later on in this book, you will come to realize that nothing in this Universe happens by accident, that every situation and event is "Elicited" by Resonance of Meaning. More on that later...

First, Dr. Moore, the Surgeon didn't tell Albert Mason, that this disease wasn't curable. Next, he didn't correct him when Mason, mistakenly identified the disease as warts. Third, Mason had great confidence in his ability to effect a healing (of warts) by hypnosis. As we explore this further, we will see that this example was a complex combination of Meanings that worked perfectly.

While under hypnosis, he told the boy that his right arm would heal, and that new soft skin would grow in its place. Because Mason really believed his suggestion, he gave meaning to the Boy that his right arm was already healing and how it would happen.

First there was the meaning of the actual disease, generated by the chemical and physical properties it contained. Then there was the Meaning of the hypnosis session that conveyed that it was sufficient to heal his right arm only, and that there would be no effect on the rest of his body.

Your power comes from your Knowing, or at least believing in your own Meanings. Mason was so convinced of his ability, that it left no room for doubt to the boy, especially since he had the boy's undivided attention while under hypnosis. Hypnosis allowed Mason to bypass the boy's natural resistance and disbelief that he could be cured. This all resulted in the miraculous cure.

However, once Mason found out that it wasn't warts, and that it was incurable, he lost his confidence in his own ability to effect a cure. He was able to finish up with the Boy, because he already had some success that proved enough to him that he could be cured.

However, when it comes to asserting Meaning while under hypnosis, it is very important that the person who is asserting the Meaning, is confident in what they are saying, because like any normal communication situation, if you are not confident in what you are saying, you will be giving off little clues in the way you say things, or the emotional content of your words etc. It will show.

When others with the same disease showed up to be cured he couldn't make it work. Because he no longer believed in his own mind that the disease was curable, so, it wasn't. It is hard to convey a Meaning that you don't believe in yourself. It always shows.

Normal Reality				A128
Physical +	Physical +	Physical +	Physical =	Physical
Meaning	Meaning	Meaning	Meaning	Meaning
of Person	Disease	Nothing Put	No Medicine	Result
	Not Curable	In His System	At All	**NO CURE**

Chapter 1

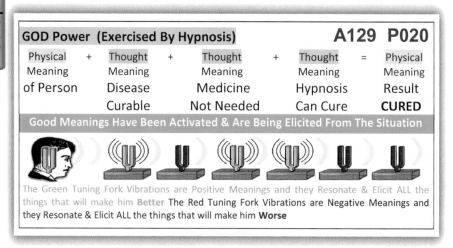

GOD Power (Exercised By Hypnosis)				A129 P020
Physical +	Thought +	Thought +	Thought =	Physical
Meaning	Meaning	Meaning	Meaning	Meaning
of Person	Disease	Medicine	Hypnosis	Result
	Curable	Not Needed	Can Cure	**CURED**

Good Meanings Have Been Activated & Are Being Elicited From The Situation

The Green Tuning Fork Vibrations are Positive Meanings and they Resonate & Elicit ALL the things that will make him **Better** The Red Tuning Fork Vibrations are Negative Meanings and they Resonate & Elicit ALL the things that will make him **Worse**

Often the meaning is more powerfully conveyed in a ceremonial setting. That is to say, the more fanfare and complexity of the way the Meaning is conveyed, the more believable it is and the more powerful it becomes. Surgery can be as much about the Meaning of being cured as it is about any real physical action that has been taken. Unlike the simple process of taking a pill, Surgery is a very involved process, of getting prepped for surgery, getting local anesthesia, and actually getting cut open and then actual things being done inside your body. How dramatic is that? You certainly expect dramatic results after all that, don't you?

Video Example
Fake Knee Surgery Works Miracles   V130

What is this video about?

This Video Example is about an experiment that was done by Dr. Bruce Moseley, Baylor College of Medicine, in Houston Texas. He rounded up a group of patients who had extremely painful arthritis in their knees. He divided them into 3 separate groups. One group would receive an actual knee operational procedure of one kind, and the second group would receive an actual operational procedure of another kind, and the third group would not receive any medical procedure at all.

He was very careful to arrange the fake operation to look just like the real thing. After the anesthesia was applied, he would actually cut the same two holes in the patient's skin as the real surgery would have, but that was all. He played a video of an actual surgery to the patient as if his knee was being operated on and the Doctor was calling for instruments and spraying water and acting as if he was actually operating. He could have won an Oscar, because his acting performance was perfect.

After a period of time, he interviewed the patients in all 3 groups and asked them if they were satisfied with the surgery. Every single patient had experienced wonderful results, even the ones who weren't operated on at all.

He theorizes that perhaps it was never the actual surgery that had been healing people, but it was just the placebo effect of having an operation done on them that was actually healing them.

The patients were interviewed 7 years later, and the successful results of the operation (or non-operation) were still unchanged. The one patient interviewed on the Video clip said that before the operation, he was unable to get around, couldn't dance and was experiencing severe pain all the time, but after the "Fake" operation, he could do anything and everything that he wanted to do, without pain.

What does this example show and what does it mean?

This is a powerful example of how Meaning can change anything. As it turns out, it was the elaborate and involved steps that have to be gone through and the high expectations of this complex procedure that resulted in a Meaning that "If you get the operation, you will be healed."

This could be considered a conditional Meaning. If he got the operation, then he would automatically get the healing. So, after the patient goes through the process and gets the operation, he has "earned" or qualified for a "Healing" status. Of course these patients weren't told right away that they had fake surgery, but instead, several years later. By that time, they were well settled into believing that they were healed, and the news of the fake surgery wouldn't cause a relapse.

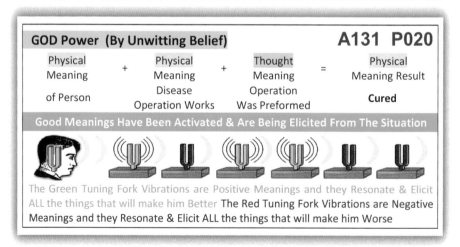

Normal Reality						
Physical Meaning of Person	+	Physical Meaning Disease Operation Works	+	Physical Meaning Operation Actually Preformed	=	Physical Meaning Result **Cured**

GOD Power (By Unwitting Belief)						**A131 P020**
Physical Meaning of Person	+	Physical Meaning Disease Operation Works	+	Thought Meaning Operation Was Preformed	=	Physical Meaning Result **Cured**

Good Meanings Have Been Activated & Are Being Elicited From The Situation

The Green Tuning Fork Vibrations are Positive Meanings and they Resonate & Elicit ALL the things that will make him Better The Red Tuning Fork Vibrations are Negative Meanings and they Resonate & Elicit ALL the things that will make him Worse

Your GOD Power Works on Anything   C132

In this physical Life Experience, you can't necessarily control or change the direction of something that is already well in process. Like if you are reading this and your House is in Foreclosure and will be auctioned tomorrow, that would be a challenge. While it wouldn't be impossible to save your house, it would be quite difficult and not really necessary. Remember, that nothing physical, nor any situation or event has any weight or effect on your experience until it has meaning. It is only the Meaning that actually "Does" anything and fortunately, you have total control over the meaning with your GOD Power.

Remembering that everything and every situation has a "Default" or starting meaning which is the basis of its existence, because if it had no meaning, it wouldn't exist. In this example of foreclosure, the usual starting Meaning is something like this, "This is all bad. I am losing my house and that represents a failure and will lead to my unhappiness." While people don't generally speak this way, meanings do. Meanings are full of conditions and results. If you neglect to use your GOD Power at this point, as many people do, you will confirm this meaning, and experience it's consequences by default.

However, if you take the time and effort to change the meaning, you will have a result, that can not only be better than the default meaning, but even better than it was when you still had your house! You can change the meaning to this, for example, "This is going to be a time of big change for me, and at this point I am free to go anywhere and even go to places that I might not have gone to otherwise, if I still owned that house. I can now entertain new ideas and I have the freedom right now, to explore all of them like never before. Since everything is always working out for me, this might just turn out to be the best thing that has ever happened to me. I look forward to this change as a new and exciting adventure for me. Bring it on!"

After changing the meaning to something like that, you FORCE, the situation to morph into a great opportunity for you rather than a great loss. It becomes the catalyst for change and growth in new and exciting ways. From this new vantage point, you will be able to see opportunities and options that you could never have noticed before from your place of depression and defeat.

With your GOD Power, you have the ability to change any situation or circumstance in your life, into the best thing that ever happened to you. No matter what happens, it keeps turning out that it was the best thing and it keeps getting better and better. But, don't forget, that not only can you change the meanings in bad situations to great ones, you can change the meanings in situations that are already great, to situations that are Amazingly Wonderful! There is no end to your ability to "Juice Up" your life experience by using your GOD Power.

C133   Your GOD Power and Physics

In Quantum physics, it is now a widely held belief that the "Observer," actually changes and affects the outcome of the event, just by observing it. No outcome can be predicted with any certainty, without taking in to consideration, the Observer who will be watching the experiment. It is the thoughts and beliefs of the watcher that is the greatest factor in the outcome of the experiment.

Video Example Quantum Physics V134

Observer Affects Outcome [6]

What is this video about?

This Video explains the difference between Energy as a "Particle" and Energy as a "Wave." It uses animation and explains what the differences are in a very easy to understand way. Particles, like marbles or electrons, act in certain ways that are different than how waves, like the waves across water or waves of energy, act in the same setting.

In this carefully planned experiment they were able to show that the results of the experiment changed and were different when they were Observed, and when they weren't. If they didn't pay attention to it, it turned out one way, but if they looked at it while it was in the process, the result changed.

(6) What The Bleep Movie What the BLEEP Do We Know - First released in theaters in 2004, WTBDWK!? went on to become one of the most successful documentaries of all time. Now distributed in over 30 countries, it has stunned audiences with its revolutionary cinematic blend of dramatic film, documentary, animation and comedy, while serving up a mind-jarring blend of Quantum Physics, spirituality, neurology and evolutionary thought. Its success has spanned a massive extended DVD set ("Down the Rabbit Hole") a companion book, study groups, a resource outlet (BLEEP Store), and a host of transformational films that continue to appear around the world. **L135**

Chapter 1

What does this example show and what does it mean?

This Video Example shows us that, what we think of a situation actually changes and affects it at its most basic and fundamental levels. We know that we can influence living things, but in this Video, we can clearly see that we can even influence the basic foundations of matter itself.

We are powerful beings with the GOD Power to change Meanings, which will change matter itself. When we look at the electron, we are thinking that it is like a particle. Our Meaning has always been that electrons were "particles." So when we watch them, with the Meaning in our minds that they are particles they change into a "Particle Formation." However, when we aren't looking at them, when we are not asserting our Meanings on them, they remain in their unlimited state of "Wave formation." In short, our expectations and Meanings have the power to alter Matter.

C136   Your GOD Power and Religion

GOD Power and Religion are naturally compatible. Most all religious faiths have said that as you believe so shall it be. That if you have the faith of a mustard seed you shall move mountains. Your GOD Power is your ability to assign Meaning to any situation or circumstance and cause it to change in a way that becomes beneficial to you. So if you believe that you have changed the meaning and you have the faith and belief of a mustard seed, then you should be able to move mountains.

Your GOD Power and Psychology   C137

In psychology, it's all about self esteem. Since your GOD Power is all about changing the Meaning of a circumstance or event, to one that makes you feel better and is in accord with your wants, desires and beliefs, then the natural result of this change in meaning will be a boost in Self Esteem. It has always been the mainstay of the self help movement to put a positive spin on every situation. To restate the event so that it is in a more positive light. This is the essence of your GOD Power. However, Your GOD Power goes way beyond, changing the meaning of a situation to just feel better; using your GOD Power you change the meaning of the situation to actually change the situation. In that regard, your GOD Power goes way beyond the low expectations of psychology from just feeling better about it to it actually causing it to work out better for real. The main difference in this work and the conventional psychology is that in psychology you are mainly focused on feeling better with no expectations of actually changing your Reality in a real way. With the use of your GOD Power, you are not only feeling better, but, you are actually changing your Reality in a very real way.

C138   Your GOD Power and Biology

Your body basically has two states: Growth or Protection. While in the state of "Growth" it is flourishing and all good things are happening. Your cells are being nourished and the best chemical signals are being sent, in short it is a perfect state of health. However, if your body is in the state of "Protection," it is partially shut down. The cells go without nourishment, your body begins to change its own genes and even its DNA exposing and even creating such traits as Cancer. It is this fight or flight mode that puts your immune system on hold. Diseases that were being held off now begin to take hold and grow. In short, while you body is in the Protection mode, everything that you DON'T WANT is happening. While you Body is in the Growth mode, everything that you DO WANT is happening. Ideally, you always want to keep your body in the Growth mode.

So how does your GOD Power figure into these two states? Perfectly! You change the state of your Body by your thoughts and perception. If you perceive the situation as a bad one, you automatically send your body into a state of Protection resulting in a cascade of unwanted results. However if you perceive the situation as a good one, you automatically set your body to a state of Growth and all the beneficial results that cascade from that state. Things that were going wrong now begin to heal, cells that need food and certain chemicals get them. Since your GOD Power is the ability to change Meaning, or how you Perceive the situation, you can always choose to perceive the situation as a good one, with possibilities and opportunities, and set your body back into the growth state of optimum health. However, if you continue to perceive the situation as a bad one, you will elicit a state of Protection from your body which will cause untold amount of damage and harm.

In the next Video Example, you will meet an amazing man Bruce Lipton, who in just the span of 7 video segments, will PROVE to you that your body does in fact respond to MEANING and as a result will always move into either a state of Protection, or a state of Growth. It can only be one or the other and it is always as a result of the Meaning of a situation, which is how you perceive it. Additionally he has the ability to explain these complex biological cell functions in such a way, that anyone can understand. It doesn't matter if you know anything about cell biology or not, after watching these Videos, it will all make perfect sense.

Video Example The Biology of Perception   V139

What is this video about?

In this Video Example, Bruce Lipton [7] describes the basics of how the cells in our Bodies operate. As it turns out, they are actually miniature Bodies themselves, with their own digestion system, nervous system, respiration system, an endocrine system, a reproductive system, an immune system, and communication system, etc., just like our bodies have.

Most importantly, he makes these points. The DNA that is in every cell has no functional power or effect. In fact, the brain of the cell is not in the nucleus, but instead in the outer skin of the cell where it decides what chemicals to activate. No matter what DNA you were born with, your cells have the ability to use whatever part of the DNA pattern that they want to and leave the rest. They even have the ability to make a completely different DNA segment and change what you were born with. You are not limited by the DNA you were born with, that was only your starting point.

Every decision that is made in the Cell, is made based on what its environmental signals are, and not on the DNA already present in the cell. Every cell has chemical receptors on its skin that are looking for the "Signals" that will tell it what it is supposed to do. If a certain chemical is in your blood stream, when it reaches the cells, it tells the cell to do this or to do that. Chemicals are Meanings and each one conveys a different Meaning to the cell. All instructions come by chemical from outside the cell. Therefore, no decisions are made based on what DNA is in the cell. The instructions from the outside tell the cell what part of the DNA to use, or to create a different segment of DNA and change itself.

The Cells basically have two main states of being, Protection or Growth. If they are in the protection mode, they are not letting in any food, they are starving. Not only are they not letting in any food, during this time, they are not spending energy or time repairing themselves. Instead they are on high alert and worrying about outside threats. If they are in a state of Growth, they are "eating" and getting the nourishment that they need, and making repairs to themselves as they are needed, and dividing when they are supposed to, and generally experiencing perfect health.

So how does the cell decide to go into a state of Protection or a state of Growth? It gets a chemical signal from you, and your thoughts. If you are worried, or upset, or any of the other "Bad" emotional states, you brain sends out the chemical signal to "Board up the hatches" and get into the Protection mode because we have a problem going on. If you are happy, feeling good about your situation, and are in a good mood, your brain sends out a chemical signal that "All is well," you can come out and play. You can all take it easy now, the threat has passed.

This means that your entire body, is either shut down, deteriorating and starving, or thriving and nourishing itself, all based on how you perceive the situation at hand.

What does this example show and what does it mean?

In this Video Example, Bruce Lipton clearly demonstrates that no matter what Genes we have to start with, it all comes down to our Beliefs as to what we will actually create in our body. You are not bound by the genes you were born with, good or bad. Everything is changeable. Your original set of Genes, are only a starting place.

No matter what Genes you were born with, your cells have the ability to create new and different genes to accommodate your perceptions, which are your beliefs and Meanings. Your beliefs and Meanings will either activate genes that you already have or create new ones that more closely match your thoughts. Importantly, he clearly explains that all of the cell's functions can be categorized into one of two groups, Protection or Growth.

(7) Bruce H. Lipton, PhD is an internationally recognized leader in bridging science and spirit. He has been a guest speaker on hundreds of TV and radio shows, as well as keynote presenter for national and international conferences. Dr. Lipton began his scientific career as a cell biologist. He received his Ph.D. Degree from the University of Virginia at Charlottesville before joining the Department of Anatomy at the University of Wisconsin's School of Medicine in 1973. Dr. Lipton's research on muscular dystrophy, studies employing cloned human stem cells, focused upon the molecular mechanisms controlling cell behavior. An experimental tissue transplantation technique developed by Dr. Lipton and colleague Dr. Ed Schultz and published in the journal Science was subsequently employed as a novel form of human genetic engineering. In 1982, Dr. Lipton began examining the principles of quantum physics and how they might be integrated into his understanding of the cell's information processing systems. He produced breakthrough studies on the cell membrane, which revealed that this outer layer of the cell was an organic homologue of a computer chip, the cell's equivalent of a brain. His research at Stanford University's School of Medicine, between 1987 and 1992, revealed that the environment, operating though the membrane, controlled the behavior and physiology of the cell, turning genes on and off. His discoveries, which ran counter to the established scientific view that life is controlled by the genes, presaged one of today's most important fields of study, the science of epigenetics. Two major scientific publications derived from these studies defined the molecular pathways connecting the mind and body. Many subsequent papers by other researchers have since validated his concepts and ideas. Dr. Lipton's novel scientific approach transformed his personal life as well. His deepened understanding of cell biology highlighted the mechanisms by which the mind controls bodily functions, and implied the existence of an immortal spirit. He applied this science to his personal biology, and discovered that his physical well-being improved, and the quality and character of his daily life was greatly enhanced. **L141**

The feeling of Fear and all of its related emotions, result in your cells activating their protective mechanisms, commonly known as "fight or flight." While in the defense mode, they fall in disrepair, and can easily become diseased. While in the "protection" mode, they activate genes and or create genes that are harmful to your health and well being. It is a toxic result of toxic thoughts.

However, the feeling of Love and all of its related emotions, result in your cells engaging in all things good. They receive the nutrition that they need. They reproduce properly, are strong and disease resistant. While in the "Growth" mode, they activate and create genes that create and promote your good health and well being.

In both of these cases, genes are activated and or created to meet your circumstance and become your true biology regardless of what genes you were born with. 95% of all cancer patients had no genes for Cancer and yet they developed it anyway.

With your GOD Power, you have total control of your body and even your genes. It is as simple as looking at your current situation and changing its meaning from, "This is the worst thing that could happen to me," to "Everything happens for a reason, and something good is bound to come of this." That simple change in meaning, changes your toxicity in your body from weakness and destruction to Growth and prospering. It not only changes the biology of your body, but it actually changes the reality of your situation.

From the place that this is the worst thing that could happen, your Vibrational resonant frequency, only interacts with more of what you see and expect to see. You can only see how bad it is and more of it. From this Vibrational place there "is no way out." However, from the Vibrational resonant place of, "There is bound to be something good that comes of this," interacts with opportunities, and options that you now become aware of. There is a way out and you can now see it. Of course it was always there, but it was just invisible to you before.

Your thoughts and their resulting Emotions fall into two categories, "Things are Going Well" and "Things Aren't Going Well." These thoughts have a chemical that represents them. The Hypothalamus converts thoughts into chemicals. It's kind of like a radio news broadcast that every cell in the Body is tuned into. If the news is bad, the chemical signal is sent throughout the Body delivering the bad news to every cell so that it can take evasive and protective action. If the news is Good, it sends a chemical message that all is well and that every cell can go about their business of growing and multiplying now that the threat has passed. These chemicals are a message of our state of being.

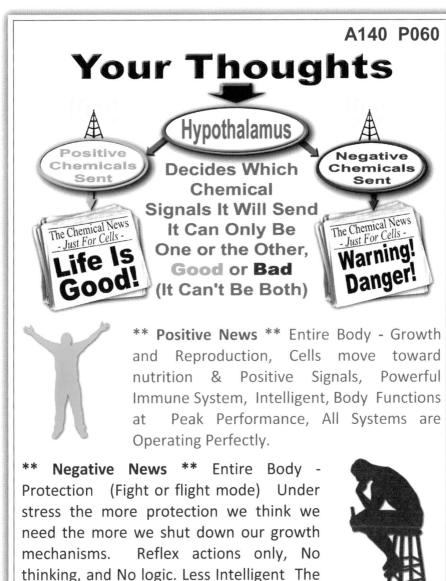

A140 P060

Your Thoughts

Hypothalamus

Positive Chemicals Sent

Negative Chemicals Sent

Decides Which Chemical Signals It Will Send It Can Only Be One or the Other, Good or Bad (It Can't Be Both)

The Chemical News - Just For Cells - **Life Is Good!**

The Chemical News - Just For Cells - **Warning! Danger!**

** Positive News ** Entire Body - Growth and Reproduction, Cells move toward nutrition & Positive Signals, Powerful Immune System, Intelligent, Body Functions at Peak Performance, All Systems are Operating Perfectly.

** Negative News ** Entire Body - Protection (Fight or flight mode) Under stress the more protection we think we need the more we shut down our growth mechanisms. Reflex actions only, No thinking, and No logic. Less Intelligent The muscles, arms and legs get the blood, Internal Organs Starve

C142   Chapter 1 Your GOD Power

- Chapter Review -

* You were made in GOD's Image, in that you were endowed with a "GOD Power," that animals do not have.

* Your "GOD Power" enables you to take total control of your life experience, by changing the "Meanings," of people, places, situations, and events in your life, at will.

* With your "GOD Power," you can do anything, from changing a Sugar Pill into a powerful cure, to building muscle, simply by watching a video and visualizing it, instead of actually having to do it.

* While your GOD Power gives you the ability to accomplish anything and everything that you can imagine, its foundation and power is based on your Belief. You must believe your "Meanings" for them to be effective.

* Your GOD Power is compatible with religious doctrine, in that if you believe that you can do it, you can. "If you have but the faith of a mustard seed, you can move mountains."

* Your GOD Power is compatible with the findings in Physics in that, it is now widely accepted and believed that, at the most basic level of our understanding, the quantum level, it appears that experimental findings are significantly influenced by the person who is observing the experiment.

* Your GOD Power is compatible with the approaches used by psychologists in that, by rethinking your current situation in a better light, you feel better about it, and you can see new opportunities where you could see none before.

* Your God Power is Ideal with Biology. With your God Power's ability to change Meanings, you can shift your entire Body at will, into a perfect state of Health and Growth.

Chapter 1 Your GOD Power   C143

- Chapter Quiz -

1) When it says that we were made in the "Image" of GOD, what does that mean?

A) We look like him

B) We can think

C) We have a certain ability/power

D) None

2) What does Your GOD Power give you the ability to do?

A) Change Meanings

B) Change Your Situation

C) Get Well

D) All

3) What do we have that animals do not?

A) Senses

B) Physical Experiences

C) Ability to Think & Decide

D) Ability to Change Reality

4) What is the foundational basis of every single experience?

A) The Actual Physical Elements & Characteristics of the Experience

B) The Underlying Meaning of the Experience

5) Does the idea of GOD Power make since in terms of Religion, Physics, Psychology & Biology?

A) Yes

B) No

See All The Quiz Answers (Page 223)

Notes - Thoughts - Insights

Chapter 2

The Meaning of Life (Your Life)   C155

There have been a lot of books written on the Meaning of Life and they address most topics that come to mind. However, this book is going to cover the Meaning of your Life starting from your choice of a physical incarnation up until you **re-emerge** back into the nonphysical realm. Your entire experience is just that, an experience and nothing more. Think of it like a "Fantasy Island [8]," the old TV show where people come to have a certain experience and the "Island" magically creates all the elements to accommodate their every "Fantasy." Like the show "Fantasy Island," there is nothing to accomplish or that needs to be done. It is only about the experience while you are here. That is the essence of your Life here on Earth. However, no matter what your "Planned Experience or Fantasy," there had to be a starting place that was appropriate to that experience.

(8) Before it became a long-running original television show, Fantasy Island was introduced to viewers in 1977 through two highly-rated made-for-television films in which Mr. Roarke and Tattoo played relatively minor roles. Airing from 1978 to 1984, the original series starred Ricardo Montalbán as Mr. Roarke, the enigmatic overseer of a mysterious island somewhere in the Pacific Ocean, where people from all walks of life could come and live out their fantasies, albeit for a price. **L156**

"Fantasy Island" (1978) Fantasy Island is a resort, where there is very little that the host, Mr. Roarke cannot provide. Thus we have visitors have adventures in fantasies that should be impossible, but this island can accommodate them such as visits to any time period they want, meet absolutely anyone they see to do something they request such as getting William Shakespeare to write a play for them. **L157**

P068

C158   Point "A" to Point "B"

When you came here to Earth, you came for the experience of being Human in Physical Form. You came for the experience of the journey from your Point "A" to your Point "B." Life is all about the journey, not the destination. When you go mountain climbing, you don't fly to the top of the mountain. You start at the bottom and experience the climb. When you go river rafting, you don't drive to the end, because it's not about getting to the end, it's about floating down the river which happens to come to an end at that point. It's always about the experience and the journey from your Point "A" to your Point "B." Point "B" is not a destination; it's the end of the experience. It is not the place you want to be, because it is the end and the journey is over.

Every Journey has an ideal starting Point "A" which will result in the most enjoyable journey, to a Point "B" which is never the objective, but, only signifies that the journey has ended. What kind of equipment you take with you depends on what your planned experience is. If you are going mountain climbing, you will need different abilities and equipment than you would need to go river rafting. Your ideal Point "A" for mountain climbing may be at the base of the mountain while your ideal Point "A" for snow skiing, would be at the top of the mountain.

When you were born, you arrived at your ideal Point "A." That was no accident nor was it chance. Nothing in the Universe can happen by accident or chance. It is impossible. However, it is possible for you to think that it was chance or an accident. That is your decision and your choice, as to what you want to believe. Your Point "A," includes the parents you chose, the financial conditions, your body type and health, your sex, your emotional and mental state of mind, the time in history, the country, the planet, the galaxy, and the three dimensional Universe that we all live in. All of this together created your PERFECT Point "A" for your intended journey and life experience. You decided and chose every single one of these aspects of your new experience. (More on that later).

Chapter 2

If your journey is to become fabulously wealthy, you wouldn't arrive as the heir of a multibillionaire. That would be like arriving at the top of the mountain for a mountain climb. Instead you would arrive at a place and time, with the ability to accomplish your way to your Point "B." It's the journey and the experience that you are here to have. People, who are born wealthy, obviously have a different journey in mind. Their Journey might be making a difference.

But remember this; everything that you do is only for you and no one else. You are the Center of the Universe and the World revolves around you. If you think otherwise, that is because of your "Immersion" into an experience that is geared to seem very Real and Realistic. However, there is nothing going on in your World that you are not aware of, even if it is on a subconscious level. You only see and experience the World that you believe in. I didn't say the World that you like, but, it is the World that you believe is real. If you think that there are really bad things going on in the World and dangers around every corner, then there are…. For You.

It's like the video game you choose. If you choose to play a war and crime video game, then in that game there are dangers and possible death around every corner. That is the game and World you chose when you turned on that game. However, if you choose a different kind of game, that is joyful, then you may find puppy dogs and bunny rabbits around every corner instead.

As you will find out in the later Chapter called The "Reality of Reality," two completely different realities can exist side by side in perfect harmony with each other. We are on a Fantasy Island, where we can have the World we choose and so can everyone else.

Chapter 2

C159   The Challenge

There is nothing that you have to get done while you are here. Everything here is only for your entertainment, enjoyment and your experience. I could give you a million dollars and ask you to give it to the most deserving and least likely person on Earth to get it, but you wouldn't be able to do it. I will warn you in advance that it can't be done. You would tell me, "I'll take that challenge." So you get on a plane and fly halfway around the World. Get in a jeep with a couple of guides and drive for days into the wilderness until you reach the base of a very tall mountain that can only be climbed. So you abandon the jeeps and start climbing the mountain cutting your way through the underbrush until you finally reach a small village at the top of the mountain. You go to the back of the village to the most rundown home, which still has dirt floors, and find a young man in the back room. You announce that you have found the most unlikely person to receive this money and you excitedly hand over the money to him.

Quite pleased with yourself you arrive back in my office to announce your accomplishment. I start smiling and tell you that despite your efforts, you have not accomplished anything special nor unusual. When you understand Resonance, you will realize that the young man had been thinking about things getting better for him, and receiving the help that he needed. He believed that it could work out for him one day in a big way. The only reason that you found him, was because he was resonating with you and attracted you to him. He was attracting wealth to him anyway, if it hadn't been you, it would have been someone else. It would have worked out for him in some way sooner or later anyway.

No matter what you do, you can't help someone that doesn't have it coming to them. They are invisible. Even if you somehow find a person like that, something will happen to deprive them of the benefit you so desperately want to provide. You can only help those who are attracting the help. And since they are attracting the help anyway, even if it's not you, it will be someone else.

The point of the story is to be sure that whatever you are doing, you are doing it because you want to do it and that you are enjoying the experience. In the example above where you traveled across the World to help that young man, if you enjoyed the experience, it was a perfect symbiotic relationship. On the one hand there was a person who wanted help, and on the other hand, there was a person who wanted to give help. That makes for a perfect experience.

However, if it was a hardship on you to accomplish the journey because you felt that if you didn't do it no one else would, think again. Everything is always working out in some way. Things have a way of evolving in the most unusual ways. Perhaps if you hadn't made the journey, the young man would have ended up moving to the big city where he might have started a program to help people and attracted many millions of dollars more than what you gave him.

Remember that we are not really physical. We are all energy trying out a physical experience for the fun of it. We came from energy and we will go back as energy and return again. This is a playground for non physical beings that came to play and experience the physical. To get in the "Game," you enter the playground by being born and you exit by dying.

C160   Name 3 World Problems

Give this some serious thought. Name three Serious World problems that we need to address as a World population or even as a nation. Take a moment right now and get at least a couple in mind before you continue.

Now that you have decided on them, I will tell you that there are no World Problems and no problems at any level. If you were to put on special eye glasses where you could see things as they really are, you would see everything on Earth and Earth itself as a swirling mass of transparent Energy. View it from space. You can see right through it like glass. It would look like the wavy looking heat coming off a hot Florida asphalt road. Using this view, let's try to "Fix" these World problems. What shall we do first? Shall we move some of that swirling energy at the surface of the energy mass and swish it over to the side over there? What do you have in mind?

If this were "Fantasy Island," when you arrived, there would be some really big disaster that needs your immediate attention to resolve. But as soon as you left, the problem would have vanished, because it never really existed in the first place. The problem was only manifested for you, because you wanted something to do, something to worry about or something to fix.

You can easily see from this view of "Reality," that nothing is going wrong. It's just circumstantial energy potential interacting with all the different resonant situations around the Globe. Like the situation with the young man and the gift of money, everything on Earth and throughout the Universe is in a symbiotic relationship. Each serves the other in some way. Because we have an environmental "Problem," we have people who love to figure out ways to help the environment. If we didn't have the problem these people wouldn't get to do the thing that they love. Doctors not only love helping people, but, also make a living at it. So if people didn't get sick, there wouldn't be a job for Doctors. War serves more people than you could imagine. There are those in the Government who love to plan the strategy, there are those who get to design and build war machines and equipment, and those who love to run around in the trenches shooting each other. If that wasn't fun, we wouldn't have played cowboys and Indians or war games with our cap-guns as kids. These are all "Camp Activities" here on Camp Earth. We are all energy beings playing physical games. Part of the fun of this camp, is the realism that we get through our "Immersion."

Immersion   C161

When we are still in our non-physical state, we know everything. There isn't anything that we can't know just by thinking about it. We didn't emerge into this Physical experience to get anything done. We came here to have a physical experience. Even though, we knew in the nonphysical what a physical experience was, there is a big difference between knowing what it is and getting to experience it. That would be like the difference between knowing about the Wild-West and actually being there in the Wild West walking the streets with your horse and your trusty rifle at your side. The experience is a million times more exciting and fun than just knowing about it. So when we arrived in the physical we became "Immersed" in our physical experience's "character," with the express purpose of having total "Realism." In order to experience a totally realistic physical Human Experience, we had to limit our knowledge and abilities to just what a physical Human has, no more and no less.

It would be like playing a part in a movie as a character in the old Wild-West. Your character wouldn't "Arrive" knowing about jet airplanes, microwaves and cell phones. He would only know about horses and stagecoaches. That would be complete "Immersion" to play the part in the old west setting. The only other difference with "Immersion" is that the character in the Wild-West wouldn't even be aware that he was playing a part. He would think that he is actually that person in that time, with those real Wild-West problems and opportunities. Complete and total "Realism," That's "Immersion."

Another way to really get the concept of immersion is thinking about a Halloween costume. You can put on a costume, with a mask and even though, people who see you on the outside may be fooled by your disguise, you aren't. You don't truly feel like the person you are pretending to be. When you reach the point, where you truly believe that you are the person that you are portraying, you have reached the state of "Immersion."

Immersion is a wonderful state of Intense "Focus." When one is in a state of Intense Focus, he may be considered "Immersed" in the projects or thoughts, where nothing else is thought of or even comes to mind. It is a highly focused concentration on a narrow range of thoughts and or work or even play.

Our experience in this Physical Universe, in this thing we call Life, is a wonderful state of complete and absolute "Immersion." This "Life Immersion" is created by what we don't know, that we don't know, and as strange as it may sound, we are further "Immersed" by what we do know. Actually, the more we know, for the most part, the DEEPER we are thrust into our immersion.

But how does something that you do know, lead to Immersion? For instance, to know about gravity and the laws of physics, is to discount and not believe anything that doesn't conform and abide by these laws. If you do know that Lead cannot be turned into Gold, any thoughts along that line are automatically blocked out, as non relevant, and of no use or not worth thinking about. So all things that you know, "Can't Be," are automatically blocked out and lead to a more focused attention and thoughts on what, can be, and what you are aware of. That is Immersion, the narrowing down of everything in the Universe to just a small range of consideration and relevance to your Human Incarnation. It thereby leads to a seemingly productive and satisfying result, due to the appropriate focus on only the relevant.

There is nothing bad or wrong about the state of Immersion. It is the Grand Design for this physical experience. It is a perfect state of consciousness to have a very satisfyingly, focused physical experience, without unnecessary thoughts directed to questions, such as, what form you will take today, or whether your car will stay on the ground, or if the project you are working on, will disappear or the surprise party you are planning has already been ruined because everyone can read your mind. Immersion, gives you some boundaries that are comfortable to abide by.

To fully understand the concept of Immersion, just consider the animal kingdom. They are even more fully immersed in their experience than we are as Humans. For the most part they only think of surviving, feeding, and breeding. They are not bothered with thoughts like, "What is the meaning of life?" "Is there life on other planets?" "How exactly, does our body work and what kind of internal organs do we have?" They have not tried to figure out electricity or why things fall. They have not complicated their day to day existence by developing a system of trade, and a system of money to exchange for goods and services with other animals. Their way of life is quite focused and immersed to a high degree. Again, there is nothing wrong with this great plan of Nature. It facilitates a very satisfying physical experience as each form of life is naturally immersed in their type of experience, perfectly.

However, Immersion, or should I say total immersion is not for everybody. For those who want to expand their experience to include super human abilities, and travel to other dimensions and all the other feats that are only a thought away, Immersion is only the starting place and not a lifelong boundary. For those individuals, the first step is enlightenment, which is the shedding of light on new areas and Ideas, which you didn't know that you didn't know.

When you don't know that you don't know, you don't even know others who do know. You are not only unaware of the information itself, but you are unaware of those who know the information, even if they are your neighbors. The subject just never comes up. But once you begin to become aware of these other areas of knowing, outside the normal boundaries of your Immersion, you start seeing and learning things that were always there but, you just didn't notice and just couldn't see them before. How far do you want to go? That is a personal decision, and it's all up to you.

C162   **Your Camp Activity**

This camp activity section is a great metaphor for your Life Experience here on Earth. When a kid goes to summer camp, he has a lot of choices of what camp activities he wants to participate in. There is canoeing, basket weaving, pottery, camping, horseback riding, bicycling, clay pot making, archery, and many more to choose from. You can't do them all, so you select 3 or 4 for the summer session.

All the activities have a few things in common. First they are all experiences. Each one is geared to be an experience and nothing more. In the basket weaving class, they don't hand you a finished basket. Instead you get to make your own basket and have the experience of making it from beginning to end. They show you how to get started and after you have learned the basics; you make your own.

Once you have chosen your activities, you are really unaware of what is going on in the other activities that you didn't choose. That is the way it should be. Whatever you pay attention to is what you are aware of. Whatever else you don't pay attention to, might as well be invisible, because you have no awareness of it at all.

If you have chosen Horseback riding, then you will always notice the horses as you pass the field that they are in because it is relevant to your experience. However, someone else who didn't choose horseback riding, nor has any interest in them, would hardly notice them, even if they passed them by on the road. The horses would just blend into the background with everything else.

The obvious thing about camp activities is that they have no real consequence, nor are they necessary. After all it is just camp which is a time to get away from home and play for the summer. What you choose to play is of no consequence, just that you are playing and having fun at what you are doing. Because, this is camp and its set up is just for the fun and experience of it, at the end of Camp, it doesn't matter if there was a basket that didn't get made or even finished, or that there was a horse that didn't get ridden, or even a mountain that wasn't climbed. So what? Nothing needed to be done or to get done. It was all just for the experience while it lasted.

This is the same with your life experience. It makes no difference what you do while you are here at "Camp Earth," because the whole place is only energy formed in such a way as to create a temporary physical experience for those who are here. Once you leave the "Camp" facility (Earth), you will return to the non physical form, from which you started. So enjoy your stay.

While here, nothing you do is for the purpose of getting anything done. Like playing in a mountain stream, at the end of the day, nothing is done, nor did it need to be. It only needed to provide an opportunity for the experience of it all. Like summer camp, there are countless possible activities that you can choose from, and no one activity is any more or less important than another. It doesn't matter whether you play the King or the pawn, this time, as it is only the experience of it that was the fun.

Like in a movie, the one who plays the King and the one who plays the Court Jester, may have an equal amount of time in front of the camera and an equal amount of lines to say, so who is to say which part is better to play? Is it playing the stuffy King who is always in a crisis, or is it the Court Jester who is carefree and always having fun? They are both valid parts and there is always a part for every player of parts. (Actors). In the end it doesn't matter what part you are playing, as long as it is one that you like and gives you "The experience of a lifetime."

What kind of "Parts" and camp activities are available on "Camp Earth?" Anything and everything that you can think of. In fact, Camp-Earth is set up in such a way so that if you can't find the part of your dreams, you can even create it.

As we know from the Challenge Example, and the Name Three World Problems Example, there is really nothing actually going on here.

Everything that is happening is doing so because there are people who have chosen it as their "Camp Activity" or the part that they want to play in this life experience. For example, take the environmental issues and the problems we face with them. Do you really think that anything could really go wrong with a planet that is formed and sustained by energy, and is populated by nonphysical beings who are having a temporary physical experience here? No, nothing is going wrong, nor can it. It is happening because there are millions of people who just love to work on solving that "Problem" as their life's work, or as I like to say, their camp activity while here on Earth. You can see how fun it must be, to figure out new ways of generating energy and inventing better devices that save energy and don't pollute, it can be very engrossing and quite satisfying.

Do you think that war is any different? There are literally millions of parts to be played in that activity, from generals to the workers at the manufacturing plant who make a living making planes, or bullets, or whatever. If playing war wasn't fun, we wouldn't have played war like games as kids.

There are doctors, who want to heal, and there are those who play the doctors and those who play the patients and there are those who play the one who lived and those who played the one who died. It's all just like a movie except that you get to really act the part and really experience it.

However, it's not your place to decide what "Camp Activities" are acceptable and which ones are not. It is no more your place to interfere in someone else's Life Experience by excluding their chosen "Activity," than it is their place to interfere with your choice. On the show "Fantasy Island," it would be totally inappropriate for someone having their own fantasy to decide what fantasies the others on the Island could or could not have. We each get to choose exactly what we want without the need for approval from anyone else. Yes, some "Activities" may be distasteful to others, and yes, society, does object to certain "Activities," but, part of choosing an "Activity," is accepting the risks and the rewards that come with it. If you go horseback riding, there is a certain risk that you may be thrown off the horse and get hurt. Likewise, if you choose a criminal "Activity," there is a certain risk that you may get caught and put in prison or even killed.

Don't pass judgment on anyone for the part they are playing. After all, in the movies there has to be somebody willing to play the bad guy, if we are going to have someone play the good guy. Like the King and the Jester, no one part is any more or less important to the whole movie. Sometimes, the bad guy part is the most significant part in the movie and the most exhilarating one to play.

The movie "Monster" that came out in 2003,[9] was about a woman serial killer who went on a killing rampage. This character was overweight, ugly in every way and downright disgusting. It was in no way a "Glamor Part." However, the actress who played the main character, the killer, was Charlize Theron. As you might know, she is a smoking HOT actress who is usually playing the beautiful leading ladies in the movies. However, she chose this part, which seemed wrong for her; after all she could have any beautiful leading lady type part that she wanted. Why did she pick this part?

When she was asked that very question she replied, "Because I wanted the experience of playing that type of role." How can you argue with that? In the end it is always about the experience. She wasn't kidding about getting the experience. She not only spoke the words and preformed the actions of the part, but, she became the part. She actually gained weight, got fat, and actually got ugly and authentically played the part for real. That is the same thing that we are doing, authentically playing a "Life" part for Real.

Charlize Theron & "The Monster"

(9) Charlize Theron & her as "The Monster" Monster is a 2003 biographical - crime - drama - thriller about serial killer Aileen Wuornos, ... Official site • Monster at the Internet Movie Database ... Monster is a 2003 biographical-crime-drama-thriller about serial killer Aileen Wuornos, a former prostitute who was executed in 2002 for killing seven men in the late 1980s and early 1990s.

Wuornos was played by Charlize Theron **L163**

Charlize Theron's Personal Web Site: **L164**

C165   **Why Do People Die Too Soon?**

Regarding children, who die young, or the like, think about this. If there were a larger than life Movie being made, and it was going to be shown to the World, wouldn't it be fun to be in the Movie? The only thing is that all the big "Speaking Parts" have already been filled. In fact, all the extras for the crowd scenes have already been cast. The only part left to "Play" in this World Famous" Movie, is one that is right at the beginning. It is not a speaking part, you will have nothing to say,

but you will be seen by the World and have the experience of being in a major Real Life motion picture. The part is only 5 minutes and it is about a person who walks out into traffic without noticing a truck is coming at full speed, and gets hit and immediately dies. The rest of the Movie is based on this person needlessly getting killed.

Do you want the part? If a part like this were available, millions and millions of people would line up to get it. Why not? You get to be seen by Billions of people. You get the real life experience of being in a movie, even if it is only for 5 minutes. You are only pretending that you are dead, because everyone knows, in "Reality," you are still alive. Why not play that part and have fun with it?

When we "Die," we only return to our nonphysical form and begin planning our next adventure. Just because the "part" was short, doesn't mean that it wasn't wanted, appreciated, and enjoyed, because it was. When Charlize Theron chose and played the part that she did, it was just for the fun and experience of it. It was a challenge to play that kind of a part as much as it is for a mountain climber to climb an unfamiliar mountain. It not only shows her commitment to her work, but it is a great example of our own Human experience here at "Camp Earth." We don't just "mouth" the words of our experience, we become the part. We are fat, or disabled, rich or poor for real. When we are trying to save a life, it's not "Hollywood," it's a real person who could really die. We get the real experience of the part that we have chosen... and we wouldn't have it any other way. Here on "Camp Earth," we get to pick our own Camp Activities and have the "Experience of a Lifetime."

Your Life in the "Planning Stages"   C166

There is nothing accidental about your life experience. You actually chose your body and planned many of the events in your life before you were even born. There was so much to choose from. In the next Video example, Michael Newton [10], a past life regression hypnotist, discloses information that he has learned about this life planning stage during our time between our physical lives. He specializes in past life regression, which is the ability to guide a person, who is deeply hypnotized back in time, before their birth, to the point that they are in a prior life.

(10) The Newton Institute was founded by Dr. Michael Newton, author of the best-selling books Journey of Souls, Destiny of Souls and Life Between Lives Hypnotherapy. Our organization began as The Society for Spiritual Regression but this name was later changed to TNI to honor its Founder. The Newton Institute (TNI for short) is the home of certified practitioners who provide the experience of Life Between Lives Hypnotherapy (LBL) to individuals throughout the world who wish to find out more about their immortal identity. Life Between Lives Hypnotherapy is a method, pioneered by Michael Newton, using a deep state of hypnosis, whereby individuals can access soul memories. For hidden within are memories of your life as a soul, between incarnations, your life with soul friends and family, planning your future lives on earth. This technique offers you an opportunity to experience a trance-induced "superconscious" state of awareness that brings a deep sense of love, compassion and an understanding of your life purpose. Everyone's experience is unique and personal so you can be confident of a spiritual journey that will fulfill your own needs and wishes. **L167**

He learned this ability to move his clients to this time between lives quite by "accident," as if there were really such a thing. One day after moving his client back to a prior life, they started speaking about their experiences during a time that was not a physical life. They were actually "Planning" their next physical life experience. They were working out the details of who they would meet, and what kinds of experiences they would have and even the body that they would use.

V168 Video Example A Past Life Regression Expert

What is this video about?

In this Video Example, Michael Newton describes his work in Past Life Regression. He accidentally got into this field of work when he was hypnotizing one of his patients and they went too far back, and ended up in a prior life experience. Since that time, he has been studying and researching Past Life Experiences and has written several Books on the subject. He has become an expert in the events following death as well as the typical experiences between lives, before people reincarnate for a new life experience.

In this interview, he answers many questions about what exactly happens in this period in-between lives. There are 5 Video Segments and I recommend that you see them all, as they are quite interesting and enlightening. I have outlined the information that I feel was most germane to our purpose.

Starting on Video Segment #2 @ 5:00, he explains that some people who have committed crimes in one lifetime may actually come back in another one as the victim by their own decision. (Remember it is all about the experiences.)

Video Segment #3 at 2:59 to 5:38, he explains the life planning between lives & speaks about "Amnesia." He says that Earth is only "one school" meaning that we can and have incarnated on many other Planets. He says that when we incarnate, we experience a sort of "Amnesia" that causes us to forget who we really are and who we have been in the past. (Of Course we know this as "Immersion")

He says that we decide on the aspects of our next life and on Video Segment #4 @ 2:00 – 7:57, he talks about our future work, and how between lives we are able to see into the future so that we can choose the right body for what we want to do. Amazingly, we choose from several different possible bodies and are able to view ourselves in those bodies in action in future situations. If we like it, then we will incarnate in that chosen body. We even choose which sex we will be in the next life and that we have all lived at least one life as the opposite sex.

What does this example show and what does it mean?

There are several great points of information in this Video Example. First, it is important to realize that we do in fact, reincarnate to experience many different Life Experiences. Remember, nothing needs to be fixed. We are only here for the experience, and not to accomplish anything or get anything done. We are only here for our own growth and personal experiences.

Next, it is important to understand that we plan certain major experiences for ourselves in advance. These experiences are not always "Happy Ones," but we have planned them for reasons that only our higher self, or inner being knows. This is important to know because the next time you experience some tragedy, you will realize that you probably had planned that for yourself as a growing experience. So get the most out of it and don't complain.

Also mentioned, is the fact that we choose the body that we will have during this particular experience. Interestingly, just like trying on some new clothes at a department store, we get to tryout our new Body in several future situations to see if it fits our personalities and what we want to experience. If we like it, we get to have it. This is important, because the next time you start to complain about your Body, know this, you picked it out for very good reasons. You didn't choose it to be unhappy, so it must have been for a very good reason, one that you may never consciously figure out during your lifetime. Suffice to know that whatever the reason, you are meant to work with the one you have. So make the best of it.

He also mentions what he calls a sort of "Amnesia," which causes people to forget who they are and their past. This is the "Immersion" that we have been talking about. While he doesn't explain why this happens, we know, that the best and only way to fully experience your "Part" (Life), is to be fully immersed into it, and only know this experience to the exclusion of all else. That is the state of "Immersion."

C169   Your "Life Painting"

In this Chapter on The Meaning of Your Life, it is important to realize that everyone is here for their own experience and not just here to facilitate yours. In this section we are going to view your life as if it were a "Work of Art." Let's take a moment and create a painting in your mind that represents your life experience, including your joys and sorrows. Include the colors that you enjoy and be sure to include what you believe and don't believe and your philosophy regarding both. What a nice work of art you have made. A life completely represented in a colorful and expressive painting.

Naturally, you weren't the only one who has been creating their own "Life-Painting." There are Billions of others who have been crafting their perfect Painting as they see fit. Like Life, their paintings are also very personal and only intended for their own individual enjoyment. People include experiences and aspects into their own painting and their own life that are their own personal choices, and rightfully so.

I have invited these Life-Painters to exhibit their Life work at a special gathering I call "Civilization." Like everyone else's painting, yours is on display in full view of millions of other Life Painters. Some of them have come over and are now asking you some questions and making disparaging remarks about your work. "Why did you use those colors on your painting? Don't you know that those are the wrong colors in the wrong place? You have way too many swirls and not nearly enough square boxes in your painting."

You are quite perplexed, because in your eyes this is a master piece. In fact it is the work of a lifetime. It is perfect in every way and quite frankly, if they don't enjoy your work, why don't they just move on to see what else is on display. After all, there is no right or wrong way to create a Life-Painting. It is a very personal thing and furthermore, the painting is only meant to be enjoyed by the one who lives it and those who can appreciate it. That is how art is supposed to be. Art is a personal creation that has no right or wrong aspects, but instead is a creation from the heart of its creator.

The interesting thing is that we give art a certain "latitude" in that we allow artist to create almost any kind of creation without undue criticism, because we know that art is an individual creation and expression, and for every creation there will be those who enjoy them and those who enjoy other art instead. The same could be said of a life. Everyone starts out with the canvas they were "Given" at birth and begins to craft and sculpt their own Life to their own taste; after all, they are the only ones who will have to live in their own creation. So why not make it a perfect fit and a masterpiece creation of a very personal nature.

These Life-Paintings, like Life, are a work in progress. You are always adding to it and making changes, to suit your ever changing viewpoints and life experience. You may notice some things that another "Life Artist" has in their Life-Painting that you really like. So add them into your Painting as well. That's the fun of an ever changing and evolving life experience. However, there may be some things that you notice in another painting that you are not fond of at all. So what? Move on. There is no need to comment, it's not your work. If you like it, incorporate it into your life experience. If you don't, then don't.

It is not our place to criticize another's life, nor their choices, because like art, it is their personal creation for their own enjoyment. Life is the most personal creation you will ever have. After all, you have this one life, (This time) so why would you, or anyone, waste a minute of it, sacrificing their own personal desires, to please someone else's opinion? It is your life-painting and your fantasy. Paint it anyway you please and enjoy your magnificent creation.

Chapter 2

C170   What is the Meaning of the Universe?

I have a definition of what the Universe is all about.

P014

> **"The Universe is Infinite Intelligence**
>
> **Expressing and Appreciating Itself"**
>
> *- Richard Lee McKim Jr. -*

The Universe is infinite intelligence, on the one hand expressing itself in as many different ways as you can imagine and more, and at the same time on the other hand, it is appreciating its own expression. For every expression, there is an equal appreciation.

First, we know that the Universe is all about new and unique expressions. That is obvious just by noticing the extreme diversity and DNA. Every single expression in the Universe is unique. Even Identical twins have different personalities and different finger prints.

Every expression has a form of appreciation for that unique expression. In example, a simple Rose, is appreciated by us for its beauty, color, and aroma, and by the bees for its nectar. Animals appreciate it, by avoiding it, because of its thorns. I'm sure that it is also appreciated by countless other forms of life and grub worms etc. However, the Whale doesn't appreciate the Rose, nor does it matter that he doesn't. But, he does appreciate plankton the food that he eats and the water that he swims in, and the Sun for keeping the water at a perfect temperature. The Earth appreciates the Sun for its warmth and the gravitational pull that keeps it from hurling out into space and supports its life.

When a particular expression is no longer appreciated, it ceases to be expressed. Like the record player, 8-track player and the Dinosaurs, it is a continual and ever evolving mix of new and unique expressions thriving in their appreciation and fading away when that appreciation ceases to be.

Chapter 2

C171   Chapter 2 The Meaning of Life (Your Life)

- Chapter Review –

Chapter 2

* You are here for a Physical Human Experience and there is noting that you need to finish or do while you are here.

* You "Arrived" in the perfect Body and in the perfect setting to start your preplanned Physical Human Experience.

* You entire Life is simply the Experience that Starts from your "Point A" and Ends at your "Point B."

* You will only be aware of and be able to help those who are attracting help. However, they will receive the help anyway whether it comes through you or someone else. So, do whatever you do because you enjoy doing it, not because it needs to be done. Nothing needs to be done.

* Every single "Activity" or "Experience" here on Earth is only for your enjoyment and entertainment. Like "Fantasy Island," the only residual importance of your incarnation, is the experience that you had and the understanding that you gained.

* There are no World Problems, much less any personal problems that are real. They are only the imaginary creations of those who are causing them and those who want to fix them.

* The entire Universe, including Earth and everything on it, are created from Energy that does not need your assistance or help, nor does it need to be fixed by you. It is only here for your enjoyment and manipulation during your Physically Incarnated Experience.

* You are immersed in this "Real-Life Movie-Like" Experience and are only aware of what is relevant to this specific experience, to the exclusion of everything else. You have no memories of past lives or the actual workings of the Universe. That would clutter up and interfere with your current and new experience that you are now embarking on.

Chapter 2 The Meaning of Life (Your Life) C172

- Chapter Quiz -

1) Your arrival here on Earth, can best be described as:

A) An Accident   B) A Well Thought Out, Purposefully Planned Event

C) A Completely Random event   D) A freak occurrence

2) In the Point "A" to Point "B" example, Your Point "A" refers to what?

A) Your Birth   B) The starting place of a journey of experience

C) A new decision   D) All of These

3) Your Physical Life Experience can be best described as:

A) An accidental result of evolution   B) Haphazard life combination

C) Playing a chosen character, that is actually experiencing their "part" as a real-life Experience

4) In the Camp Activity Example, it states that you are here for what?

A) To experience the activities of your choice

B) To get something done that needs to be done

5) The concept of "Immersion" can best be described as:

A) The complete and utter focus on your physical experience to the exclusion of all else

B) Remembering your nonphysical abilities and your history from before your birth

See All The Quiz Answers (Page 224)

Notes - Thoughts - Insights

Chapter 3

The Most Powerful Formula in Your Life   C184

The "Platinum Formula"

This most powerful formula is:

> *"Everything Is Working Out For You If You <u>Know</u> It Is."*
>
> *R.L.M.*

P010

Chapter 3

Each and every word in this formula has an important meaning, so, we will break down this amazing formula into its different parts to get a full understanding of the power that it holds.

"**Everything**" means all aspects of your Life experience. Everything that you can think of and is important to you is covered by this formula. Your health, Love life, social life, financial well being, happiness, work, hobbies, and everything else you can think of. If it is important to you, and even if it is not, this formula covers it.

"**Is**" means right NOW, in the present. Not in the future, right now, at this very moment. This doesn't mean going to be, or eventually. It means RIGHT NOW, AT THIS VERY MOMENT, it IS happening.

"**Working Out**" means whatever events, actions, occurrences, are in the process are all successfully occurring. Regarding your Health, it might mean that your body is successfully healing itself and maintaining its health. Regarding your financial situation, your business and efforts are paying off bringing you the money that you need and want. Regarding Happiness, you are experiencing it and you are finding joy in everything. It means that whatever "Everything" is to you, it is working out successfully for you.

"**For You**" means that this applies specifically to you, for you, and no one else. While things may or may not be working out for others, they are definitely working out specifically "For You." This is because this formula works in terms of the individual or groups who embrace it. This part is a little tricky because this formula has a "Condition" attached to it. So, individually, you can easily meet the condition. However, sometimes it is more difficult for a whole group to meet the condition.

"**If**" means that there is a "Condition" attached to this formula. You get to enjoy all the benefits of the formula, including that it encompasses everything that you want, that it is all working out for you right now, only "If" you meet the condition following the "If." If you do not meet the condition stipulated, all the Valuable benefits thus far outlined will not be Guaranteed, nor will they even occur. You MUST be not only willing to honor and fulfill the condition attached; you MUST be dedicated to it.

"**You**" means you specifically and no one else. It MUST be YOU who acts on this formula. No one else can act on your behalf. It is only YOU who can initiate this formula and activate it to your benefit. Since your life is guided by your own thoughts, that "you can only notice what you think about," and that "you can only see what you notice," and that you can only choose from what you notice, it makes no difference what anybody else thinks. No matter what anyone else thinks or is thinking, it cannot effect what you notice or don't notice. It is impossible. Only You can light up the World that you notice and see.

A good example of this might be two people looking at a huge parking lot full of cars. The first person is thinking about red cars the second person is thinking about a different color. The first person who is thinking about red cars notices them all over the parking lot and what the second person next him is thinking is of no consequence what so ever. You can easily see that whatever color the second person is thinking of, cannot influence what the first person is noticing. However, if the second person says

"I am thinking about how many White cars are out in this huge parking lot." Then the first person would not only notice the red cars, but he would begin to notice the White cars as well. Interestingly, since the second person never learned what color the first person was thinking of and noticing, the second person is still only noticing the white cars.

I must point out that if you listen to, and give thought to, the opinions of others, good or bad, it will influence the World that you will notice and see, not because of what they were thinking, but, because of what you are now thinking. You will subsequently notice and see, what they were noticing and seeing. This is not wrong, it's learning. By reading my words, you are listing to me right now, and hopefully, my words and thoughts will influence the World you experience in a good way.

"Know It Is" means that you have an absolute certainty about it. Many people would substitute the word "Believe" in the same place. However, I draw a clear distinction between these two words. Believe aspires to be Knowing. Belief is good and it's strong, but, it's only tentative Knowing. With belief you have strong confidence in it, but in the face of strong opposition to it, you may experience some doubt. It could cause you to feel less confident. That is the nature of Belief. However, with Knowing, there can be no doubt.

Chapter 3

If I were to ask you "Will the Sun rise tomorrow? Even if you only have the most basic understanding of our solar system, you would quickly answer with a resounding "Yes," to that question without any hesitation. That answer comes from a place of Knowing, where there is no doubt nor is there even the possibility of doubt. It would be almost impossible for me to convince you that the Sun will be taking tomorrow off and won't rise again till the following day. That is "Knowing."

Another example of Knowing, might be your Name. You know what your name is and anyone would be hard pressed to convince you otherwise. However, if you got a call from a case worker or some hospital worker, or even a conversation with your Mother, who told you that your real name is actually different on your Birth Certificate, it might shake your confidence in what your real name is. Or if you are a woman who got married and you were told that your Last name hadn't actually been changed on the necessary documents, that might cause some doubt. However, if you had seen the documents yourself, your confidence would be unshakeable, and you could state emphatically from a place of knowing that your name is correct. However, If I asked you what name you go by and respond to, you would definitely answer that question with certainty as there is no possibility of doubt, no matter what any official papers may say.

The odd thing about this Formula, is that if things are working out for you, you of course you know that they are and this formula quickly becomes useless. After all, who needs a special formula to simply state the obvious? The power of the formula is that things will always be working out for you when you know that they are, and they always are. You just have to KNOW it. Not just believe it, but KNOW it.

There was a time when people didn't know for sure that the Sun would rise again. In fact, they didn't even Know that the Earth was round and not flat. However once they Knew for sure that the Earth was round and that the Sun had to rise every day, then, it became Knowing, and could never be lost again.

Likewise, when you reach the level of "KNOWING," that everything is working out for you in every way, at all times, then everything WILL actually be working out for you, at all times and in every way. The rest of this book is dedicated to giving you the information that you will need to reach KNOWING. Like the ancient civilizations who through knowledge, reached a level of Knowing, which could never be taken away, so you too will gain this permanent state of Knowing, that will catapult your Life into never ending happiness and joy. Because you will always KNOW that everything is working out for you, as a result, it WILL always be working out for you.

We will revisit this powerful formula at this end of the Book when you will have enough KNOWING to use it effectively.

Let the Quest for KNOWING continue....

Chapter 3

Chapter 3 The Most Powerful Formula In Your Life

C185   (The "Platinum" Formula)

- Chapter Review –

"Everything Is Working Out For You If You Know It Is."

* The "Platinum" Formula is the most powerful understanding of Reality that you can have or will ever need.

* The "Platinum" Formula is only about you and cannot ever be applied to anyone else.

* The "Platinum" Formula is only effective if you KNOW that it is true and that it works.

* The "Platinum" Formula Will work your entire life

Chapter 3 The Most Powerful Formula In Your Life

(The "Platinum" Formula) C186

- Chapter Quiz -

"Everything Is Working Out For You If You Know It Is."

1) In this formula, what does "Everything" refer to?

A) Your Finances

B) Your Personal Life

C) Your Health

D) All of Them

A186

2) In this formula, what does "Working Out" mean?

A) Getting Better

B) Staying The Same

C) Getting Worse

D) None

3) In this formula, who is "Everything Working Out" For?

A) Your Neighbor

B) Your Best Friend

C) Your Mother

D) You

Chapter 3

4) In order for this formula to work, who has to be the one who "KNOWS" that everything is working out?

A) Your Neighbor

B) Your Best Friend

C) Your Mother

D) You

A187

5) What does it mean to KNOW something?

A) You're Doubtful

B) You Wonder About it

C) You Hope it is

D) You are Certain

See All The Quiz Answers (Page 225)

Richard Lee McKim Jr.

Part II

Frequencies & Resonance

C198

Notes - Thoughts - Insights

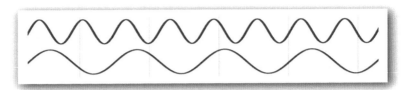

Chapter 4 Frequencies & Meaning   C199

Everything in the Universe is energy. All energy Vibrates. The way that meaning shapes Energy, is by causing a certain "Frequency" that forms the energy into matter or circumstance. It forms it in the same way that a certain frequency will form a musical note, or form the color Red. In music, we listen to a certain range of frequencies that we can hear. In that range, a certain frequency will "Form" a certain sound that we can actually hear. A combination of frequencies together, will form a song. In the Light spectrum [11], there are a certain range of light frequencies that we can see. If the light is in a certain frequency, we see red light. If it is a combination of different light frequencies, we see a picture.

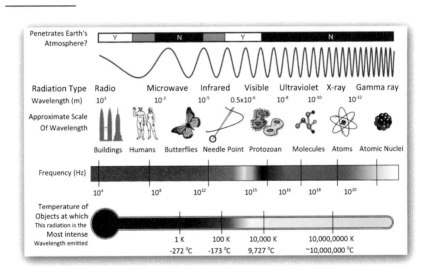

(11) The electromagnetic spectrum is the range of all possible frequencies of electromagnetic radiation. The "electromagnetic spectrum" of an object is the characteristic distribution of electromagnetic radiation emitted or absorbed by that particular object. The electromagnetic spectrum extends from below frequencies used for modern radio to gamma radiation at the short-wavelength end, covering wavelengths from thousands of kilometers down to a fraction of the size of an atom. **L200**

If we have a certain combination of light frequencies in combination with sound frequencies, we can watch a movie of an event or the actual event as it is happening. It is all a matter of different frequencies in combination. It's important to understand how frequencies added together create a new single frequency that is made up by a combination of other frequencies.

In the Video Example below is a visual demonstration of how a sound frequency can form a shape and pattern out of a pile of rice. It is only the sound frequency that is acting on the rice. Frequencies have a powerful ability to form Energy into everything from matter to situations.

V201   Video Example Frequency Creates Shape

What is this video about?

The first demonstration is by a device sitting on a table. It is a Vibrational devise that has a sheet of metal sitting on top of it which is about 18 inches by 18 Inches square. They pour quite a bit of Rice on top of the sheet of metal before they start it vibrating. Naturally, as you would expect, the rice is just in piles, randomly poured over the sheet.

As they turn on the vibrating device to a certain frequency, it transmits the vibration to the sheet of metal, and an interesting thing happens. The Rice begins to form patterns over the metal. Where the Rice

"Accumulates" is the place where the frequencies meet and cancel each other out. They are the "Nodal" lines where an up frequency meets a down frequency and end up canceling each other out completely and equally causing a "quiet" area where the Rice can remain without being vibrated all over the place. The other areas where two up frequencies or two down frequencies meet become very "noisy" and are a place of extreme vibration. No Rice can remain in that very Vibrational place long.

What does this example show and what does it mean?

What this video example shows us is that Frequencies have the ability to cause formations and patterns. Every bit of matter in the Universe is made of Energy that has a certain Vibration. Each certain vibration creates a certain thing. Vibrations are what form energy into the different elements and particles that the Universe is made of. This example shows that a certain vibration will form a certain pattern in the Rice. As the vibration was changed to different frequencies, it resulted in different patterns.

Chapter 4

99

V202   Video Example Frequency Creates 3 Dimensional Shape

What is this video about?

This video shows a low frequency speaker with a Corn Starch Mixture. As it vibrates, the Corn Starch begins to take a three dimensional shape by rising up into the air. This shows, that even a sound frequency has the ability to form and shape matter, if the conditions are right.

This is the explanation that was posted with the Video.

"Corn starch is a shear thickening non-Newtonian fluid meaning that it becomes more viscous when it is disturbed. When it's hit repeatedly by something like a speaker cone it forms weird tendrils. The video was shot at 30 fps and the speaker cone was vibrating at 30 Hz which is why there is no blur. This is the original video with the actual sound of the speaker."

What does this example show and what does it mean?

This Video Example just shows that a sound frequency can not only create a two dimensional pattern, like we saw with the rice, but can actually create a three dimensional form as well. Of course, these frequencies are very low frequencies at the sound level. The actual frequencies that form matter, and are the basis of creation, are outside of our ability to notice them. Just like infra red light frequencies, we know that they exist, but we can't see them.

Chapter 4

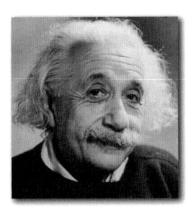

Frequency Is the Genius of Creation   C203

I have always found that the simpler a concept or design is, the more intelligent it is. Using Frequencies to shape energy is the Genius of Creation. It is so simple and yet so powerful. However, you just don't realize how amazingly intelligent and powerful it is until you give it some serious thought.

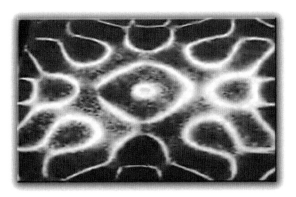

Consider the picture of the Rice pattern above. Look at it very closely for a moment. Pretend that you are talking to a friend by phone and you want to describe this particular pattern so that your friend is able to recreate that same pattern with some rice. How would you begin to describe this pattern? Would you have to measure it in inches or millimeters? Where should the lines be thicker and thinner? Exactly how thick or thin should the lines be? How would you describe the exact arching curves and where they begin and end? What language would you use? What words would you use? Flowing? Arching? Curving? Connecting? Enclosing? Separating?

Chapter 4

It is such a simple pattern, and yet, it is so difficult to describe and replicate exactly. Yet, the Universe can recreate that pattern, every time, again and again, just by using a certain frequency. It is so much easier to transmit a Frequency that describes an abject or a situation, than it is to use any other method. It works so well, because the entire Universe is energy, and that's the one thing that energy is really good at, Vibrating. Can you imagine the Universe having to describe over and over again how to make a Hydrogen Atom, or a Water molecule in any other way? Instead, if you want an Oxygen Atom, just use the Frequency pattern that Means Oxygen. It's like the fact that you can be defined by the "pattern" of your DNA. Your DNA is the physical expression of a certain Frequency that Means "YOU."

Imagine a musical band. In this band there is a singer, a drum player, a piano, a lead guitar and a base guitar and a trumpet. Each of these instruments, including the singer, puts out its own set of frequencies that are changing, but within the range of that instrument. A drum puts out a different range of sound than the guitar or the trumpet, and definitely different than the singer. But when they create a song, it has its own frequency as a whole, even though it is made up of many different frequencies put together.

That is the essence of matter. It is composed of molecules, which are composed of atoms, which are composed of electrons, neutrons, and protons, which are composed of yet smaller parts all of which have their own frequency at their level of existence. Just as the guitar has its own frequency, it is part of a song, which is part of a movie, which is part of the theater experience, which is part of a Person's individual experience and it just keeps going and going.

Chapter 4

However, even if you are in the movie theater, watching the movie, with all the dialog and action, you can still listen for and hear the sound frequency of the guitar playing in the song playing in the background of the scene. Even though the Frequencies are more complex, they still contain and are able to Represent all of their basic elements. Nothing is ever lost in the "Whole." When you listen to a song, as a single Frequency, you can still experience and recognize any of the individual instruments that make it up.

That is a basic understanding of frequencies and how they are gathered to form greater and yet greater situations and objects. The Universe is made up of first, energy, formed into smaller particles than we will ever know at a certain frequency, then after many untold levels, finally form electrons, neutrons and protons, (Which is where we begin to understand the Universe) which then form atoms, all of which have their own frequencies at their own level. Then eventually they form molecules, and matter, and planets, and solar systems and Universes. While they each have their own frequency and "Song," they are also adding unto the greater and bigger picture until it becomes the Universe. And, just like the different sound elements of a song come together to form one song, all the elements and frequencies of the Universe come together to form The Universe, "One-Verse."

Chapter 4

C204   Chapter 4 Frequencies & Meaning

- Chapter Review –

* Frequencies are second only to Energy as the basic Building Blocks of the Universe

* Meanings create Frequencies which causes Energy to Vibrate at certain Rates

* Frequencies Range from the highest Vibrations which are unseen and immeasurable, to the Lowest ones which can be seen as Light, heard as Sound, and Felt as Movement.

* Frequencies are added together to form more and more complex frequencies

* Frequencies have the power and ability to form energy into matter and circumstance

* Frequencies are the Genius of Creation because they convey so much information

* The Entire Universe is a single Very Complex Frequency know as the One-Verse

Chapter 4

Chapter 4 Frequencies & Meaning   C205

- Chapter Quiz -

A205

1) Frequencies and combinations of Frequencies are the basis of what?

A) All Matter   B) All Circumstances

C) The Universe   D) All

A206

2) What is the basis of a Frequency?

A) Meaning That is Already Present   B) Meaning That You Assign

C) Either

3) Frequencies can be added together to form:

A) More Complex Frequencies   B) Matter

C) The Universe   D) All

4) Frequencies Form What into Matter and Circumstances?

A) Energy   B) Stuff

C) Corn Starch   D) Rice

5) The essence of a Frequency is That it Causes Energy to:

A) Become Circumstance   B) Vibrate

C) Create Form   D) All

Chapter 4

See All The Quiz Answers (Page 226)

Notes - Thoughts - Insights

Chapter 5

Chapter 5 Resonance, The Secret   C217

"Match-Making" Force Of The Universe

So, now that we know the Universe is made up of combinations of frequencies forming Energy into matter, situations, and events. We also know that it is Meaning that creates these Frequencies. So, what is Resonance and what does it have to do with Your GOD Power? What does "Resonate" mean and how is it the "Matchmaker of the Universe?" Well you know what GOD Power is and what it does. But, now, I'm going to explain to you how it works through Resonance.

Frequencies have an amazing quality, it's called Resonance. Resonance happens when similar frequencies are in proximity to each other. If you had two equally tuned guitars in the same room, and you plucked the third string on one of them, did you know that the third string on the other guitar would automatically start to vibrate? That is called Resonance. Resonance elicits an automatic response from like frequencies. If there was a piano in the same room and it had a string that was the same frequency to the one that you were plucking on the guitar, it would also respond automatically by vibrating on that string of similar frequency.

If you played a Music CD on your stereo system, that was of a person plucking the third string on a guitar, the third string of a guitar in the same room would still vibrate, because it is not responding to the first guitar, but instead to the frequency that it is generating. It would respond every time whether the frequency vibration is coming directly from the guitar, a stereo system or something else.

Chapter 5

This quality of Resonance, is so amazing and powerful and yet so it is so easy to use. It will add greatly to your KNOWING of how the Universe really works. Did you notice that I said it elicited the response and the response came automatically? The other guitar did not decide to respond, it automatically responded. Also, the other guitar did not respond on its own, the response was "elicited." Called forth, beckoned, commanded, requested. The other guitar, not only responded, but, it had to respond, it couldn't decide not to. It responded exactly when it should have and with exactly the appropriate "Tune," vibration, and frequency. The other guitar did not respond with a different "Offering" or a different frequency, or on a different string. It responded with exactly the perfect match to the frequency it heard. Furthermore, there was no effort on the other guitar's part to respond. In fact, no one plucked the string on the other guitar, it responded by itself, "Plucking Itself" so to speak, effortlessly, automatically, and appropriately as it will and does every single time.

The same thing would happen, if you plucked the first string on the first guitar. It would cause the first string on the other guitar to vibrate in automatic response. The same resonating effect would happen if you plucked the last string; it would automatically elicit the identical response from the other guitar. That is the quality of Resonance. This is the fundamental basis of the Universe.

Also, when the other guitar begins to respond, it makes a sound and a vibration. Because of this, it catches your attention and stands out from everything else in the room. Interestingly, not only does it catch your attention, but, you catch its attention also. After all, you are causing it to vibrate and respond to you, what more do you need to get its attention? In a situation of Resonance, each not only becomes aware of the other, but due to "Likeness" they each are attracted to each other. Thus, the "Law of Attraction."

The property of Resonance not only works with guitar strings, but it will work with Tuning forks, drums, and anything that makes a sound. If you struck the bottom of a kitchen pot or pan, the sound it made would be the exact frequency required to Resonate with it.

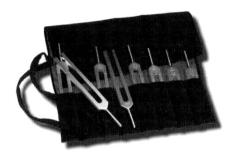

The next Video Example uses "Tuning Forks," to demonstrate the principle of Resonance. They come in different sizes and different frequencies. Tuning Forks act just like a Guitar, when one tuning fork is vibrating at a certain frequency, and another one of the same frequency is nearby, it starts to vibrate also, automatically. To further understand this special quality of frequencies check out this next Video Example.

Video Example
Tuning Forks Demonstrate Resonance   V218

What is this video about?

In this video, Grandpa John [12] has two Tuning Forks that are each mounted on a special chamber that makes the sound that they are emitting be able to be heard. The tuning forks are the silver colored metal objects sticking up into the air from the tan colored rectangular wooden sound chambers. A "Tuning Fork," is a cast metal device shaped like a very long "U." They are formed to certain lengths that result in different frequencies when they are struck by a mallet. They are used as a reference to tune instruments, because they are always at the exact frequency.

_____

(12) Grandpa John **L221**

Chapter 5

Guitars and pianos and the like, get out of tune as their strings stretch over time. So tuning forks are used to tune them to the exact frequency they are supposed to be at. Since the tuning fork never gets out of tune, it can be used for years and years without needing to be replaced.

In this demonstration, he strikes one of the tuning forks that are mounted on the sound chambers. Immediately, you hear the sound that that tuning fork is making. However, that sound is not from just the tuning fork that was struck by the mallet, but instead from both of the tuning forks mounted on the sound chambers. The frequency caused by the first one, causes the second one to start vibrating and create a sound also. It is most important to note, that the second tuning fork, which is now vibrating and producing a sound of its own, was never touched in any way. It just automatically started vibrating as soon as it "Heard" the other one vibrating. That is the quality of Resonance.

Once the second one starts vibrating and making a sound, which was immediately after the first one started, he picks up the first one by holding the forks. This stops them from vibrating and making any sound. However, you still hear the sound because the second one is still vibrating.

He then demonstrates that it can go either way. So he strikes the second one first this time, and the same result is experienced, except that it is the first one that is now "Responding by Resonance." Like the first time, he picks up the one he struck, (the second one), and still the first one is still vibrating.

As a final demonstration, he takes out two other tuning forks that are made to create two different frequencies. He strikes them and neither of the first two tuning forks responds. Even though they are not mounted on a sound chamber, they would still have responded if the frequencies were a match. This demonstrates that resonance only occurs when there are "like" frequencies involved, or devices that vibrate at like frequencies.

What does this example show and what does it mean?

This Video Example, shows in a clear and understandable way, what resonance is. From this example, you can easily visualize the guitar strings responding to each other in resonant fashion. This video points out the two most important things to remember about Resonance.

First. Resonance occurs only in the presence of "Like Frequencies," and will not respond when the frequencies are not a match. Second, the response is automatic, and requires no additional energy, nor does it need any physical action on your part. It is a natural function of nature. Resonance is so automatic, that it would respond in a glass box where no one could touch it, as long as the sound vibration reached it. The resonant "Effect" will continue as long as the primary vibration is activating it.

It is very important to understand that Resonance causes a "MUTUAL" awareness and activation of the "Like" Frequencies. It would be like a guy at a party looking to meet other people like himself. So he shouts above the noise of the crowd, "I like Fishing!" Suddenly, there are several other people in the crowd who then shout back, "Me Too!" They end up coming over and they start talking about Fishing.

When he shouted that he liked fishing, he was transmitting a certain Frequency out into the World around him. As he did this, those who had a similar "Likeness" (Liked Fishing) responded in the same way with the SAME Frequency. He elicited their response by sending out something about himself. They didn't respond by saying that they were hungry or that they wanted to dance. If he had shouted, "I like Ball-Room Dancing," he would have had a very different result. If there were anyone in the room who also like Ball-Room Dancing they would have responded, but the ones who liked Fishing would have remained quiet and unmoved. They would not have Resonated with that Particular Frequency.

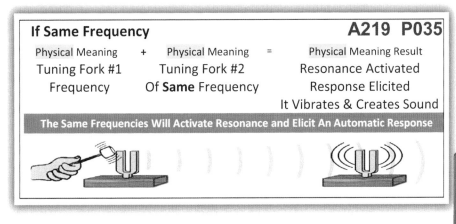

If Same Frequency		A219 P035
Physical Meaning + Physical Meaning =		Physical Meaning Result
Tuning Fork #1 Tuning Fork #2		Resonance Activated
Frequency Of **Same** Frequency		Response Elicited
		It Vibrates & Creates Sound

The Same Frequencies Will Activate Resonance and Elicit An Automatic Response

Chapter 5

When you start the first one vibrating at a certain Frequency, the vibrations reach the second Tuning Fork of the same Frequency and then Resonance causes it to start vibrating also. The Frequency Vibrations from the second one now come back to the first one and begin a Resonant action between the two of them.

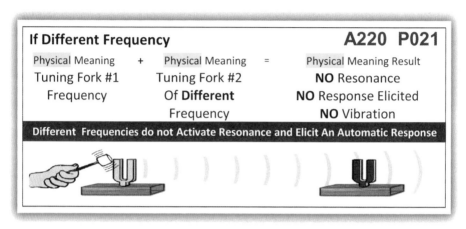

If Different Frequency		A220 P021
Physical Meaning +	Physical Meaning =	Physical Meaning Result
Tuning Fork #1	Tuning Fork #2	**NO** Resonance
Frequency	Of **Different**	**NO** Response Elicited
	Frequency	**NO** Vibration
Different Frequencies do not Activate Resonance and Elicit An Automatic Response		

C222   Resonance in Real Life Situations

Now that you have actually seen Resonance in action with your own eyes and ears, let's get back to our guitar example. What would happen if you plucked the third string on the one guitar and the other guitar didn't even have a third string? Nothing happens, and nothing can happen. If the other guitar doesn't have a string that vibrates at the same frequency, it does not "Hear" the first guitar, it is totally unaware of it, and as a result it does not respond in any way. You could pluck the third string on the first guitar until your fingers bled, and still, there would be no response coming forth from the other guitar. Resonance only responds "In Kind." It has to be a like frequency to elicit any response. This is very important to understand.

Resonance is not only a "Pervasive Force" that is everywhere and always in action, but it's a very POWERFUL force as well. In the Video Example below, the wind blowing through the cables on the Tacoma Narrows Bridge [13] caused an audible sound which just happened to match the Resonant Frequency of the Bridge. Even though the bridge was made of steel and concrete, and must have weighed thousands if not hundreds of thousands of tons, the simple sound that the wind made caused that massive structure to writhe and twist as if it were a child's toy being tossed around.

How much "Real" force would have been required to lift that massive bridge into the air like that? How many cranes and jacks and the like would be needed to shake that bridge as forcibly as that sound did? I don't even think that we have anything that I know of, that is big enough and powerful enough to lift and shake that bridge like that simple sound was able to do.

It is important to note, that it wasn't the wind blowing against the bridge that caused this result. You could stand in a 42 mile and hour breeze. You can visualize how strong a 42 MPH breeze is by thinking of yourself standing up in the back of a pickup truck that is moving at 42 miles per hour. It's nothing. It would have to be a wind in the hundreds of miles per hour range to move that bridge in that way. But just a simple sound at the right frequency, can elicit a powerful response.

---

(13) Galloping Gertie **L223**

Chapter 5

V224   Video Example Resonance Rips Bridge Apart

What is this video about?

This segment is a video of a bridge twisting and ripping itself apart. This is a famous video that was taken in Tacoma Washington in 1940 by Barney Elliott, and his friend Harbine Monroe. [14] The suspension bridge was built very strong and lasted until the day came when the wind was blowing at just the right speed (42 MPH), which caused a sound when it passed through the cables holding the bridge up.

The frequency of the sound was just exactly the right one, and matched the resonant frequency of the entire bridge. As we know, the bridge began to respond to the call of Resonance by twisting and shaking and bending until it ripped itself into pieces causing it to finally stop vibrating. After a large part of the bridge fell into the river, and the bridge was now in two pieces, its resonant frequency was much different and there was no longer a resonant effect going on.

What does this example show and what does it mean?

What this example shows, is that everything in the Universe from the very small to the very large has a resonant frequency that is the result of every single aspect of its makeup including size, shape, materials, and even non physical qualities such as thought and meaning.

(14) <u>Camera Shop Tacoma</u> **L226**

When you cause a frequency that matches with anything, it will activate it and command it to respond in any way that it can, even if that is by twisting and jumping until it breaks apart. It WILL RESPOND EVERY SINGLE TIME IT GETS THE CALL in the form of a vibration that resonates with it.

As you can see in the video, at 1 minute and 9 seconds, they show the bridge from a wide angle view, and there are people just standing around watching the bridge. There are a few bushes in the scene that are hardly moving at all. It is not the power of the wind that is twisting this bridge, it is the power of the exact frequency that results when cables are at the right tension and the wind is blowing by them at just the right speed, like a bow strokes the violin strings. If the wind had been faster or slower, the bridge would have been saved.

Resonance is a powerful force when you know how to activate it. It will respond every single time and work day and night for you. It will always get a response and it will always work.

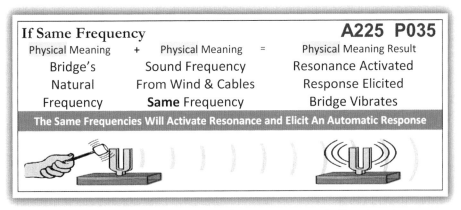

If Same Frequency		A225　P035
Physical Meaning　+	Physical Meaning　=	Physical Meaning Result
Bridge's	Sound Frequency	Resonance Activated
Natural	From Wind & Cables	Response Elicited
Frequency	**Same** Frequency	Bridge Vibrates
The Same Frequencies Will Activate Resonance and Elicit An Automatic Response		

Resonance was achieved by the wind causing a sound vibration that was an exact match with the structure of the bridge. They responded to each other by vibrating. The wind had its vibration represented as a sound, and the bridge vibrated by physically twisting. This is a great example of a "Physical-Resonance."

In the next Video-Example, we will see the old, "sound breaking a wine glass" demonstration. When a resonant frequency reaches the glass, also in the form of sound, the glass shatters because it cannot flex enough to respond to the resonant frequency. The frequency is demanding more of a response than the glass is capable of.

Chapter 3

V227 Video Example Resonance Breaks Wine Glass

What is this video about?

This Video Example is a demonstration of how a Resonant frequency can affect an object that vibrates at the same frequency. This demonstration is in a lab setting. There is a wine glass which is to be the target of the demonstration. There is a frequency recording device and a powerful amplifier with a speaker attached. Additionally, because the movements of the glass will be so fast, and at such a high frequency, they have mounted a strobe light above the glass so that it, in effect slows down the motion to the point that you can actually see it.

Using the microphone on the recording devise, they tap the glass with a stick to cause it to make a sound. That sound is the resonant frequency of that glass. In other words, based on the actual material of the glass, and on its shape, with all factors considered, it has a certain frequency that it vibrates at. (Just like a guitar string that is a certain thickness, a certain length, a certain tension etc, results in a certain frequency that it responds to, and at the same time, is the same frequency which is the note that it will play when strummed.)

After the resonant frequency of the glass is determined, the same exact frequency is set on the amplifier and it is turned up very loud. The speaker is next to the glass sending the exact same frequency that the glass made when it was tapped. Amazingly, the glass begins to quiver and actually flexes and bends to the sound. I don't know how solid glass could bend as much as it does, but after a while it is no longer able to bend enough to respond to the sound and it shatters into pieces.

What does this example show and what does it mean?

This was just like the old commercial many years ago that had a famous singer singing and it shattered a glass. What happened is she hit the high note that matched the glass and unlike a guitar string that can vibrate and move quite a bit without breaking, the solid glass couldn't flex enough and it shattered.

What this example shows is that when a resonant frequency is matched, it must respond. The glass has no choice but to start to vibrate and flex to the sound that is like it. Resonance is a POWERFUL force. It demands a response to likeness and the response always comes willingly even if it means that it will shatter itself doing it. There is no denying the call of Resonance.

This is why, if you set your thoughts and beliefs clearly on what you want, you will elicit, no, let's make this clear, YOU will DEMAND a response from the Universe, commanding everything like YOU, to show up and respond to you. There is no choice. It will shatter itself in order to respond to your call. People, situations, events, places and things, will go out of their way and cooperate with you as they respond to your Vibrational invitational call.

However, if you are not in Vibrational accord with what you want and are looking for, there is nothing you can do to get any response what so ever. Opportunity will not only be invisible to you, but you will be invisible to opportunity. It will go on without you and around you and behind your back and there will be nothing you can do to stop it.

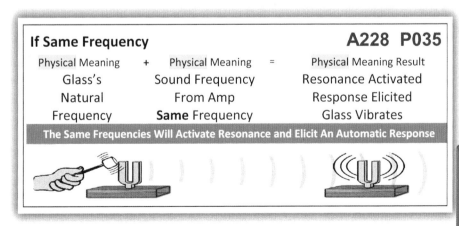

If Same Frequency		A228 P035
Physical Meaning +	Physical Meaning =	Physical Meaning Result
Glass's	Sound Frequency	Resonance Activated
Natural	From Amp	Response Elicited
Frequency	**Same** Frequency	Glass Vibrates
The Same Frequencies Will Activate Resonance and Elicit An Automatic Response		

Chapter 5

Resonance is not limited to physical things. Situations also have a frequency that can be resonated with. In the Video Example below, a waitress in a customer service situation mimics the customer's exact words, causing a resonant quality between them. This ends up eliciting a better tip from the customer.

V229   Video Example
Resonance Helps Waitress Make More Money

What is this video about?

This Video Example is from a show called "Weird Connections" on the Science Channel. In this segment of the show, they are doing an experiment to see if a waitress can make more money in tips if she repeats exactly what her customers have told her.

The experiment is done in the normal scientific manner, where there is a "control group" of waitresses who are told do not repeat what the customer has told you, but, you can write it down and perform your duties as usual. The experimental group of waitresses is told to always repeat everything the customer says when they are ordering, exactly as the customer has said it.

As the experiment concludes they find that on average, the "Control Group" receives an average tip of half a Euro while the Experimental group, receives on average one and a half Euros. This is three times more money in tips, just because they mimicked the customer's exact words.

What does this example show and what does it mean?

What this Video Example shows is that when a person deliberately takes action to be "Like" someone else, they create a situation of "Likeness" which is a Resonant quality. When you are in a resonant relationship, you are able to elicit better cooperation and a higher level of friendship. Likeness is so powerful, that salesmen are often taught to mimic a customer's movements called "Mirroring" to gain a deeper connection with him resulting in making more money. This video shows that Resonance has the ability to elicit the desired results from situations just by being alike. Neither waitress group worked any harder than the other nor did they provide any better service. It all came down to only one thing, being "Like" the customer in a way that created a resonant quality, that elicited a greater and better response, easily and automatically.

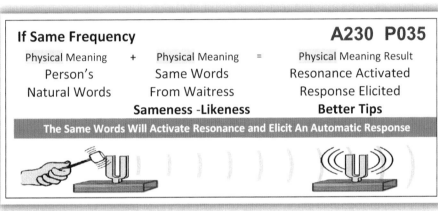

Resonance has been shown in a Physical way with the Bridge and the wine glass, and in a relationship way between people with the waitress experiment. However, Resonant qualities are not limited to those two ways. Resonance can be experienced in any situation. In the Video Example below, a computer agent gives a persuasive speech to college students to keep their student ID with them at all times.

At first glance, the computerized head has nothing in common with the student. They are not saying words back and forth like the waitress, and there is no sound frequency that is being matched between them like the Bridge and the Wine Glass. So what can the computer simulation do to attain some sort of "Likeness" or resonant quality that will help the agent achieve his intentioned purpose which is to influence the Students?

In the Video Example, the computer "Agent" achieves a resonant quality by matching the students head movements. It is an amazing result, but not surprising, that a simple identical movement of the head is enough to achieve a resonant quality, or "Likeness."

Chapter 5

V231   Video Example Resonance Helps
Computer Agent Be More Persuasive

What is this video about?

This Video Example is also from the show called "Weird Connections" on the Science Channel. In this segment of the show they are doing an experiment to see if a computerized head, an avatar, can influence a college student by mimicking their head moments.

The experiment is done in the normal scientific manner, where there is a "control group" of students tested where the computerized head just moves in a way that has been preprogrammed and has no relation to what the student is or is not doing. However, with the experimental group of students, the students' head movements were tracked and mimicked exactly by the computerized head 4 seconds later after the student moved their head. (They found that 4 seconds was the perfect time so that the students didn't catch on to what was happening.)

The computerized spokesman was trying to persuade the student that it was a good idea to carry your student ID card at all times on the college campus with all the reasons that supported that position.

As the experiment concludes they find that on average, the "Control Group" was not particularly persuaded by the argument, while the group who had their very own head movements mimicked, were much more influenced by and agreed more often with the ideas presented.

Chapter 5

Every other aspect of the experiment was exactly the same, the speech was exactly the same, and there were head movements by the computer spokesman regularly in both cases. The only difference was that in the more persuasive result, the head movements happen to correspond to the student's own head movements at a 4 second delay. All other factors remaining exactly the same, "Likeness" is persuasive on its own.

What does this example show and what does it mean?

What this video example shows is that when a person is in a Resonant state with "someone" they elicit a cooperation, a response that is favorable, and in accord with that in which they are in resonance with, even if the other person is a computer avatar.

This shows you that you can resonate with anything that is like you in any way. It can be like the way you move your head or like the way you speak, or like the way you sit. But, most importantly, you resonate most powerfully with people, situations and events that are similar to your thoughts and beliefs.

This example just shows you that "Likeness" does catch your attention and causes a REAL effect that can be seen and measured. If you "Tune" yourself by controlling your thoughts and beliefs, and keep them where you want to be, You will be the one causing the resonant effect on all those around you who are like what you are being and wanting to be. You will be the one who elicits the favorable responses and results from your World.

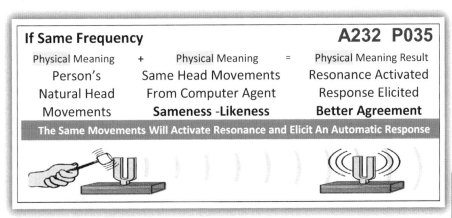

If Same Frequency		A232 P035
Physical Meaning + Physical Meaning =		Physical Meaning Result
Person's	Same Head Movements	Resonance Activated
Natural Head	From Computer Agent	Response Elicited
Movements	**Sameness -Likeness**	**Better Agreement**
The Same Movements Will Activate Resonance and Elicit An Automatic Response		

Chapter 5

C233   The Guitar Store

So, now that you understand what Resonance is and how it works, how do you use it and how does it work with Your GOD Power? We will be using a Guitar Store as a metaphor that represents your World. We will say that the high strings on the Guitars, play the "good notes" and represent good things and the low strings play the "bad notes," and represent bad things. The higher notes are the better notes. So you enter a guitar store that is huge, in fact, it is as big as the Universe. There are hundreds of thousands of guitars everywhere. They are on the shelves, the walls the ceiling, hanging in the air and everywhere you look. This guitar store not only has new guitars, but they also sell used guitars, some in good shape and others that are broken, out of tune and even missing some strings. Some even have the strings in the wrong place. In this store, like the Universe, you can find anything that you are looking for.

You step up to the guitar salesman and say, "I am just looking for the guitars that are able to play the high notes, the good things, just the best ones. Do you know which of these guitars can play those high notes?" The salesman smiles because he hears specific requests like this one many times a day. He responds, "There is no way that I can keep track of which guitars can play what notes. Additionally, what I think is a high note may not be a high note to you. Taste is a very individual and personal thing. No one else can choose for you. Only you can choose for yourself. Also, due to changing conditions, any one guitar that could play the high notes yesterday, may not even play them today, and vice-versa. You will have to find what you are looking for on your own."

So, this guitar store is a metaphor for the Universe, and the Guitars themselves are the people, places, events and situations that exist in the Universe. Like guitars, people, places and events, have certain frequency combinations that make up what they are about. So, how do you choose from everything that is in the Universe, and pick just the right the circumstances and events that you want from all that is available? As in the real World, it would be impossible to check each and every guitar, person, place, thing and event in the World individually, just to see which ones are a "Match with you." There must be a better way to sift through everything in the World and get just what you want. If it were you in the Guitar store, what would you do?

Did you think, "Use Resonance, the Universal matchmaker?" If you did, you are correct.

Just so we can understand this concept better by visualizing it, let's modify all the guitars in the Guitar store, by adding a little devise that will turn on a light when any of the strings on that guitar are vibrating. In other words, if I were to pluck the third string on my guitar, and the other guitar with the Light-Device on it, has a third string in tune with mine, it would automatically start to vibrate. And since one of the strings on the guitar was vibrating the light would turn on, for as long as the string was vibrating. This way we can visually "see" which guitars are in Resonance with us.

Here is the solution. The easy way to find what you are looking for is to cause it to stand out from the rest of the World. The way you cause it to stand out and catch your attention is to elicit a response from it and cause it to resonate with you. First, turn out the lights in the Guitar store so that you are not distracted by "Good Looking" guitars that cannot perform the high notes. Then, play your own guitar on the exact string and note that you want.

You walk the walk, talk the talk, and "be," think and do the things that you want to see in your World. As you play the exact note that you want, all the other guitars that are capable of playing that same note begin to respond automatically. There are guitars lit up all over the store, as a result of being in resonance with you. You notice them and they notice you. Resonance is a mutual attraction. As you look around in this metaphoric world, you see beautiful houses that are exactly what you are looking for. There are great jobs everywhere. You can see that the economy is booming and opportunity abounds. There are fabulous vacations, people, places and things everywhere. As you play your high string, you vibrate a wonderful feeling of all is well, and it always works out for me and there is opportunity everywhere. You are eliciting the very best that the store has to offer.

Chapter 3

In this moment of pure bliss, you wonder "Aren't there any bad things out there in this World because I don't see any of them." The answer is Yes, they are out there in the World along with every possibility and combination that you can think of, but you can only notice what is in resonance with your thoughts. In this guy's situation, he is vibrating, thinking, talking and walking a great frequency and vibration, and as a result, he only notices the good things that are a match with his thoughts. So the answer is Yes, they are out there, but he can't see them and neither can you. They are in the dark and invisible to him. From where his current vibration is, he is unable to notice and see anything else.

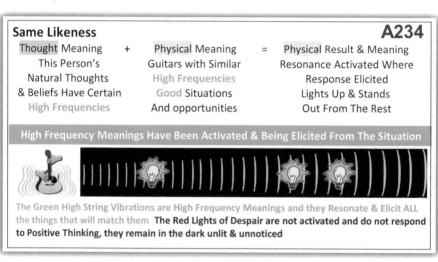

Same Likeness   **A234**

Thought Meaning	+	Physical Meaning	=	Physical Result & Meaning
This Person's		Guitars with Similar		Resonance Activated Where
Natural Thoughts		High Frequencies		Response Elicited
& Beliefs Have Certain		Good Situations		Lights Up & Stands
High Frequencies		And opportunities		Out From The Rest

High Frequency Meanings Have Been Activated & Being Elicited From The Situation

The Green High String Vibrations are High Frequency Meanings and they Resonate & Elicit ALL the things that will match them **The Red Lights of Despair are not activated and do not respond to Positive Thinking, they remain in the dark unlit & unnoticed**

After he selects what he wants from the opportunities that have made themselves known and presented themselves to him, he stops playing that wonderful note in order to enjoy his findings and selected experiences. Just then another gentleman comes in the store. He obviously is quite upset and without prompting he begins to play the lowest string available on his guitar as he speaks. "What an awful day that I've had already. My car broke down, I can't find a job in this bad economy, I got sick, I'm behind in my house payments and it's just getting worse all the time. It's going to get a lot worse before it gets any better for me. But, I am looking for a guitar that plays the high notes, just the good ones that will make my situation better. Do you have any?" The guitar store owner responds as usual, "You will have to choose for yourself, it's not my place to select one for you, only you can see the guitar that is the right Match for you."

As this new guy looks around, he sees lights everywhere. These are all the guitars that are in resonance with him. But not with what he wanted, but, instead with the vibration of his real thoughts. He may say that he wants the good things, but all he is focused on and talking about and thinking about is "Low String" bad things. So, as a result all these guitars that are lighting up, are the ones that are capable of resonating on the low strings and playing the low notes. He is eliciting the worst guitars that the store has to offer. As he looks around in this Metaphoric World, all he sees are bad things. He says "Look at that one, no jobs are available, and I knew it. And look over there at that news report; foreclosures are at an all time high. I can't see any opportunity out there for me. I knew it. I just knew it."

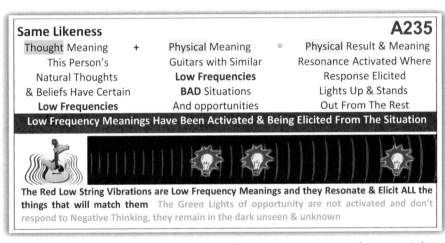

Same Likeness		A235
Thought Meaning +	Physical Meaning =	Physical Result & Meaning
This Person's	Guitars with Similar	Resonance Activated Where
Natural Thoughts	**Low Frequencies**	Response Elicited
& Beliefs Have Certain	**BAD** Situations	Lights Up & Stands
Low Frequencies	And opportunities	Out From The Rest
Low Frequency Meanings Have Been Activated & Being Elicited From The Situation		

The Red Low String Vibrations are Low Frequency Meanings and they Resonate & Elicit ALL the things that will match them The Green Lights of opportunity are not activated and don't respond to Negative Thinking, they remain in the dark unseen & unknown

As we all know, there are actually opportunities and great jobs everywhere "out there," but because of how he thinks, he doesn't notice them because he is in resonance with the lack of opportunity. He literally cannot see them. Even when they are right in front of him, they are invisible. They are in the dark, out of sight and out of mind.

Then as they finish talking a third man enters the "Guitar store of life" and just like the rest, he requests the best guitars that are available. Once again, the guitar store owner tells him that he is the only one who can find what is a true match for him. It might not be exactly what he wants, but it is "what is available to him." He can only choose from what he is aware of. He is only aware of what he notices, and he only notices what is in resonance with him and catches his attention. After all, you can only choose from what you notice and become aware of. How could you choose something that you can't see or don't notice?

Chapter 5

So, like the two customers before him he begins to play his own guitar and talks at the same time, matching his words with his tune. Then like the others, lights begin to appear in the dark, indicating resonance and likeness with him. He starts out by saying "I'm a realist. I tell it just like it is the good and the bad. I know that there are lots of wonderful opportunities out there just waiting to be noticed." As he was speaking, a whole bunch of lights appeared out of nowhere. He continued, "But, I also know that the World is full of pitfalls just waiting to swallow up a man and take every cent that he has." More lights appeared as he said that. "There is some of everything out there and it's just a crap shoot as what you end up with." Even more lights appeared. Now the guitar store was lit up like a Christmas tree. The only problem was… "Which guitars were capable of playing the high notes and which ones were total losers? After all, he thought and talked about good things and bad things and lit up some of everything. This is where most people are.

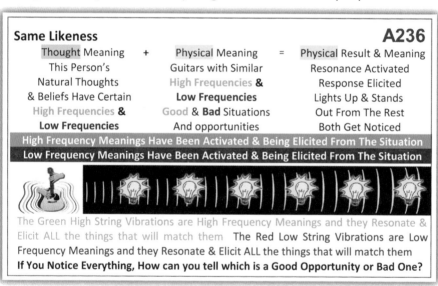

Same Likeness		A236
Thought Meaning +	Physical Meaning =	Physical Result & Meaning
This Person's	Guitars with Similar	Resonance Activated
Natural Thoughts	High Frequencies &	Response Elicited
& Beliefs Have Certain	Low Frequencies	Lights Up & Stands
High Frequencies &	Good & Bad Situations	Out From The Rest
Low Frequencies	And opportunities	Both Get Noticed

High Frequency Meanings Have Been Activated & Being Elicited From The Situation
Low Frequency Meanings Have Been Activated & Being Elicited From The Situation

The Green High String Vibrations are High Frequency Meanings and they Resonate & Elicit ALL the things that will match them The Red Low String Vibrations are Low Frequency Meanings and they Resonate & Elicit ALL the things that will match them
If You Notice Everything, How can you tell which is a Good Opportunity or Bad One?

The first guy only played the high notes that he wanted and therefore, only elicited from the Universe, responses that matched what he wanted. It didn't matter what opportunity he chose, because everyone was a winner and blessing to him. However, with the second guy, it didn't matter what opportunity he chose, because every one of them was a loser and would lead to more heartache. However, with the third guy, he elicited a little bit of everything.

Chapter 5

That's like working in a gold mine that is also a mine field. You don't know if the next call you get is a great new job offer or a call from the Doctor with bad news about your health.

So, how do you use your GOD Power, to elicit only what you want? Well first, remember that Your GOD Power is the power and ability to assign Meaning to any person, place thing, event or circumstance and you elicit and resonate from that Meaning. So you start by assigning the good meaning that everything is working out for you in some way. Every situation no matter what it is or how it looks, is leading you to a better situation and the Life that you have always wanted. Affirm to yourself that opportunity abounds and can easily be seen by those who know it's there. As you assert these meanings, you will cause a vibration within you, a frequency that elicits a "like" response from your life experience through the power matchmaker of resonance. You will begin to notice and see anything and everything that you ever wanted. And while you may not get the thing you want instantly, you will notice the path that will lead you there.

So, how is this using your GOD Power, because it sounds just like positive thinking? The difference between using your GOD Power and using Positive Thinking is your level of consciousness. Your God Power is a higher consciousness function. That is to say, that you have awareness, that when you assert meaning, you actually create a resonant force that causes the Universe to respond by eliciting what you want and making it stand out, and become available to you. You KNOW what you are doing and have a high expectation due to simple cause and effect. While positive thinking on the other hand, has good intentions, and usually makes you feel better, you don't have the conscious awareness that you are deliberately forcing the Universe to create favorable options for you.

If you didn't take the initiative to use your GOD Power to assert the new meaning in an otherwise bad situation, you would be eliciting all things bad. You could only notice how bad things are and how they are getting worse. I've got news for you, not only do things look bad from that perspective, but, they are bad and getting worse for real.

Just too really get this point VERY CLEAR. Let's revisit our example of the man who died by the Placebo effect. Remember, he had a very negative view about the future of his health. So, not only did things look bad for him from that point of view, BUT, they actually were bad. He elicited his own death as a result of his poor point of view. So, your point of view affects more than just how things look and seem to be, it has the power to make things actually happen, good or bad.

So, if nothing is working out for you and every path that you take leads to a dead end, then you have to do something about it. You can't let that continue, or it WILL GET WORSE. It has to, it is the power of Resonance to elicit and bring you more. You have to say and think a different meaning instead, such as, "This is just making me stronger. Every no, is one step closer to the yes I'm looking for. This could be the day that an amazing opportunity comes my way. Every day is full of possibilities that could lead to the life of my dreams." When you change the meaning of your situation, you change your vibration, and as a result, the doors that were invisible before, suddenly are not only noticeable, but they are wide open, and inviting you to a new world of opportunity and success.

If the "starting" meaning of your situation is desperate, for example, then you would think of a new point of view and assert a new Meaning such as, "This is the beginning of Great Things." If this is NOW the beginning of Great Things, then you now expect to elicit from the Universe these "Great Things." After all, if this is NOW, the beginning of great things, there must NOW be Great Things to be found. That is the deliberate and conscious use of your GOD Power. You assert the new Meaning, and then look for and notice the results that you have elicited and will be eliciting from the Universe.

Just remember, if you are looking for red cars, you will see them everywhere. And if I ask you how many white cars did you see, you will be unable to answer, because you were not noticing them. They did not catch your attention because they were not on your mind. When you think that nothing is working out for you, all you can see is that which verifies it, and nothing is working out. Even if there is an amazing opportunity right in front of you, you will not notice it, and therefore not see it, you will not be able to choose it. It will be in the dark and invisible to you.

The "Meaning" of "Meanings"   C237

It has come to the point where we need to really understand how powerful and versatile Meaning is and why it is the Basis of Creation. Many people equate Meaning to Definition. That is they say that the definition or description of the object is its Meaning, but that is not exactly correct. Some might say that Beliefs or Intention somehow equate to and describe Meaning, but that is not exactly right either. Meaning is much more powerful and fundamental than definition or Intention as they are very different slices of "Possible Reality."

Meaning vs. Definition: If you look at the picture above, you might be inclined to say that it is a pencil and that it is a writing instrument. You would be correct, that is, as far as defining it, in its most limited sense. But what if I asked you what is the "Meaning" of what you see above? Then what would you say? If you "Defined" a placebo as a fake sugar pill used to fool patients into believing that they have taken REAL medicine, you would be correct. But is it the Definition of the pill that saved the patient or was it the Meaning of the pill? Meaning and definition are quite different. What is the Definition of "Foreclosure?" What is the Meaning of "Foreclosure?" While the Meanings could range from the worst possible thing that could happen to a new freedom full of possibilities, its definition would still be the same.

In the picture above, an art teacher might assign the meaning to it that it was a sample of what the color Yellow looks like. To a Geometry teacher it might be an example of a multi-sided cylindrical object. To a botanist, it might be an instrument that pokes holes in the ground to plant seeds. To a trapper, it might be the trigger mechanism on his trap. To someone with a wobbly table, it might be a shim that keeps the table from moving. It could just be a "Picture" representation of the real thing. It could have hundreds of meanings but it still would only have one definition. Since Resonance is a Function of Meaning, you can easily see how many different possible ideas and results could be elicited from the Universe as the Meanings changed from one thing to another. That's why Resonance is based on the Meanings and not the Definitions.

Chapter 5

Meaning vs. Intention: Intention is not Meaning either. If your house is in Foreclosure, what is the Meaning of that? The Meaning of it and your Intentions about it are completely different concepts. Meaning is a "Primary Force in the Universe." Intention is not.

While people talk about the power of Intention and all that, it is actually a weak position and has little or no power compared to Meaning. Since Meaning is the Primary Force in the Universe, it always comes first in any situation or circumstance. First a situation has Meaning, THEN you may or may not have certain intentions about it after that. Just to be clear,

"You Cannot Have Intentions About Something If It Does Not Already Have Meaning"

How can you have an intention about something if you don't know if it is a good situation or a bad one?

Meaning is present FIRST, then comes whatever your intentions are about it. However, if you control the Meaning in the first place with your GOD Power, then of what use is Intention? If you have changed the Meaning to "This situation is working out," then what would your Intentions need to do? Nothing. The situation is already working out. You are already eliciting positive results from the Universe based on what the situation now Means. The situation is "Solving Itself." You are already eliciting everything that is needed to AUTOMATICALLY cause this situation to evolve into what you want all by itself.

Intention is a "Responding" function that is in some way responding to whatever Meanings are already present. Intention is only useful if you don't use your GOD Power to change the Meaning. Then you could have the Intention to make the best of it, or whatever. BUT, why take the weak position of "Responding" to the Meaning already present, when you can just go ahead and change the Meaning to a more favorable one with your GOD Power? If you just go ahead and change the Meaning to a better one, then you don't have to worry about "Intending" anything. It just starts working out all by itself after that.

When Intention is used in an initiating way such as "I Intend Peace on Earth," it is like wanting. Whatever you "Intend" for yourself or about another, or the World for that matter, is the same as wanting but, a bit stronger and more assertive. There is nothing wrong with this because, like "Wanting," it brings to mind these thoughts so that they can

Resonate with your World and Elicit the relevant results. But, it is easy to see that "Meaning" and "Wanting" are completely different concepts. If you have the Meaning that the pill you just took is a Miracle Drug that will cure you, it will. But if you "Intend" or "Want" the pill you just took to cure you, it is not nearly as certain.

When Intention is used in an initiating way such as "I Intend to have a good day today," you are saying in a Meaning way that it is possible that you might not have had a good day otherwise. You are asserting in a Meaning way that your "Days" aren't naturally or automatically good on their own. What if you have an accident on the way to work? What would that do to your "Intention" to have a great day? From this place you may feel that your day has somehow gone bad or been temporarily interrupted. Now you will have to Respond to this new development because it does not meet your initial "Intention." Would you then "Intend" to make the best of it? If you even for a moment thought that you are going to make the best of it, you are asserting the Meaning that it is a bad situation that you have to somehow "Cope" with or get past. So, if its Meaning is that it is a bad situation, be prepared to elicit some negative results, regardless of your "Intention" to make the best of them. This is because the "Intention" to make the best of them, asserts that they are bad in the first place and that they do exist.

Why not assert the Meaning of "My days are always great and everything is always working out for me in every way," instead? Then if you have a accident on the way to work, you know that this is STILL working out for you in some way and that you are still eliciting the best results from this new situation. From this place, you will notice the new options and opportunities that are now present. It is always good and getting better all the time.

When you ask the question "What does this Mean?" the answer you get is in the present, right now. It is not something that is wanted or going to be later. Resonance and the Universe is acting on that Meaning right NOW. Meaning is a complete and "Finalized" condition or state of affairs. Intention on the other hand is not finalized. It is still "Going To Be." That is, it "Intends to Be." But, it is not there yet, because if it was, it would be Meaning. When you say that the pill IS a powerful Cure, it is. It is final. There is nothing more to accomplish or to happen. It is NOW a powerful drug that will cure you. However, if the same pill "Intends" to

Chapter 5

be a powerful cure, it is not there yet. But it makes big promises on what it "Plans" on doing, or "Intends" on becoming. How will you know if it actually "BECAME" a powerful cure as it Intended to do? Is it a wait and see kind of thing? What if it didn't make it? Would you rather the Doctor tell you that this Pill IS A POWERFUL CURE, or that it Intends to be and that it is planning on it? Meaning IS, Right Now in the Present. Intention looks toward a future time in which what was Intended will become experienced or actualized. In this way it is sort of like a "Goal."

Meaning vs. Beliefs: Meanings are different than Beliefs in very subtle and yet important ways. Once again, Meaning is a "Primary Force in the Universe." That means that it comes FIRST before Belief. You MUST FIRST have established the Meaning, either by assessing the Meaning already Present or by asserting one of your own creation, then and only then, comes Belief in the Meaning which then empowers it.

While Many people would substitute Beliefs for Meaning, they are fundamentally different. Most people, which includes me in many places throughout this book, will refer to a person's Meaning as a Belief. Technically Meaning is a certain Understanding and Position regarding the object, situation or person etc., then your degree of Belief is your level of confidence in the Meaning. Belief is more specifically confidence and your assessment of a situation's validity.

In Example. You might Believe that the Situation will work out in a very positive and beneficial way. You might say that is your "Belief," and it is, but, technically, your Meaning is that it is working out just fine for you and you have high confidence in that Meaning. You Believe it.

Just to give you another example to show you how these two concepts are truly different, even though most people, including me, put them together. When something happens and you say "I don't Believe this!" you have assessed the Meaning of the situation and you have given it a very low confidence level. No Confidence. No Belief. You wouldn't now call this one of your "Dis-Beliefs" would you? You don't go around talking about you "Disbeliefs" because you don't think of them in that way. It isn't wrong to call the Meanings that you believe your "Beliefs," I just want you really understand exactly what Meaning is and how it is separate from Beliefs, but still integral to them.

Resonance and Quantum Physics   C238

Physics is divided into two main categories which are "Classical Physics," and "Quantum Physics." The "Classical Physics," is used to describe large objects from billiard balls to Planets, while "Quantum Physics," is used to describe the motion and activity of very small particles such as electrons.

The first of these, "Classical Physics," is described as "Billiard Ball Physics." This is the Newtonian view of matter in that it is the study of physical matter interacting with physical matter. When this ball hits that ball at a certain speed and a certain mass, the second ball will move in a very predictable manner every single time. This level of physics has described the Universe, our Planet, and the interaction of matter very well for hundreds of years and more. For our purposes, this level of Physics is the understanding and description of the Physical "Representations" in our Universe. Remembering that nothing really exists in the physical, but instead it is only "Represented" there. So, Classical Physics describes and explains these "Representations." This would be a certain amount of energy that is represented as a "Billiard Ball" hits another certain amount of energy representing itself as another "Billiard Ball," which results in certain new positions that these representations will assume after the interaction. As we know these representations are created by Meaning, and can be changed if their Meaning is ever changed. Thus, water can be changed into wine or rocks into Bread.

It is at this level of consciousness and understanding that matter seems real. It is at this level of understanding that our eyes receive light through the lenses and convert them into electrical chemical impulses in our brains into an image. That is the "Classical View of Physics," that everything really exists and that situations and circumstances are real physical events that MUST always respond in a certain way.

Chapter 5

In this way of viewing the World and our Universe, we easily predict that if a person has their eyes closed, or they have no eyes at all, then since the light is unable to reach the visual cortex by the system of electrochemical impulses, the person is unable to see. It is from this physical Representational view, that we know that fire burns flesh, and that missing hands are unable to feel objects. It is in this view that we are accepting the already established Meanings of objects and situations. In this View of "Reality," a bullet with a certain weight or Mass that is traveling at a certain speed, will penetrate flesh and cause a severe wound as a result.

Remembering that our own Realities will always support our own point of view, the view point of "Classical Physics" has been verified and substantiated for hundreds of years. Even when there was evidence to the contrary, it was never scientifically provable evidence, it couldn't be replicated, it was discounted, or it just never came to the attention of the main stream physicists.

Now, we get to the very interesting and most important of these two view points of physics. The second level of Physics is known as "Quantum Physics," which deals with the activity and interaction of the most fundamental elements and particles of our Universe. At this level, nothing is certain. No actions can be predicted at all. All that "Quantum Physics" can predict is "Possibilities." Nothing is certain and instead, everything is possible.

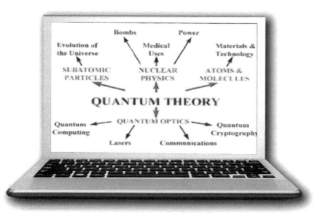

Video Example

V239   Quantum Physics & Consciousness

What is this video about?

This Video Example features two of the most prominent thinkers of our time who are expressing their views about Quantum Physics and the Nature of Consciousness. Amit Goswami, Ph. D. [15] says:

"Quantum Physics enables us to see directly that we can make sense of the World ONLY if we base the World on Consciousness. The World is made of Consciousness. The World IS Consciousness. Consciousness is the ground of Being. Quantum Physics makes this as clear as daylight."

This means that the World is not only created by Consciousness, but it is sustained and maintained by Consciousness as well. Consciousness creates by Meaning. Meaning is the foundation of the Universe. We cannot predict the event, only the possibilities. So what determines the specific outcome from all of the possibilities? He continues by saying that,

"Consciousness MUST be involved. The Observer cannot be ignored. The Observer is part of the description of the World."

We realize that consciousness is more fundamental than objects. That means that Consciousness is at a higher level and has domain over matter. He continues by saying:

"The mathematics shows us clearly that the movement of objects are describable only in terms of possibilities, not the actual events that happens in our experience. Only Objects can be described mathematically and only to the extent that they are Possibilities."

(15) Amit Goswami, Ph.D. Theoretical Quantum Physicist Professor Emeritus of physics at the University of Oregon's Institute of Theoretical Science, Dr. Goswami is a revolutionary in a growing body of renegade scientists who in recent years have ventured into the domain of the spiritual in an attempt both to interpret the seemingly inexplicable findings of their experiments... and to validate their intuitions about the existence of a spiritual dimension of life. A prolific writer, teacher and visionary... Dr. Goswami has appeared in the movie "What the Bleep do We know?", The "Dalai Lama Renaissance", and the recently released award winning documentary on his life and teachings: **L240**

Chapter 5

Quantum Mathematics can only prove that it is possible that the objects exists. This means that noting is absolute because at any moment it could be changed by a new and different meaning. It is Consciousness that is in control of and directs matter.

If we lived in a Real Truly Physical World where matter was a real physical thing, then it would be easy to prove again and again that a rock is a rock. But since the Universe is a creation of Consciousness in the form of Meaning, it is only a rock at the moment and its Meaning could be changed at any time to something else such as bread or gold. So for the first time, Science encounters free will, because the outcome depends on the choice of the Observer and that cannot be predicted scientifically. Amit says:

"Then we see that the Chooser is free. There is freedom of choice and of that Freedom of Choice comes our actual experience."

This is YOUR GOD POWER! The chooser always has freedom of choice. He can decide and assign any Meaning he chooses to any situation, event, or object that he wants, and from that Meaning, that choice, comes his resulting experience. Your Experience is "Elicited and Created" from the Meanings that you give it.

Professor of Physics, Director of the Institute of Science & Technology at M,U,M. John Hagelin, Ph. D. [16] says that it is clear that "Consciousness is not created by the Brain." He says that the Entire Universe and everything in it are Alive and Conscious at the very core. It is a Field of Dynamic, Self Aware Intelligence from which all things emanate.

He says that: *"The deeper you go in the structure of natural law, the less material, the less inert, the less dead the Universe is. The more alive, the More Consciousness the Universe becomes. We are really living in a thought Universe, a conceptual Universe."*

What does this example show and what does it mean?

This is a wonderful Video Example that proves that nothing is certain. Nothing is already settled. There is always a sea of infinite possible outcomes or possible transformations available. As these two prominent experts on Quantum Physics so aptly put it, "Nothing is final and certain until the Observer makes a choice." That is to say, the

Observer decides and asserts a Meaning to the situation or event. At the moment that the situation or event has a Meaning, a specific outcome is chosen and elicited from the sea of all possibilities by Resonance. You might say that Resonance takes the Meaning and goes out and "Extracts" the perfect and most appropriate outcome for that Meaning.

P028

Quantum Physics is the Science of How Observers and their Meanings Create and Affect the Outcomes of Events.

R.L.M.

Once a Meaning has been created, it Resonates with the Universe and elicits a specific Response, which is then called the "Result or Outcome." For once, it is completely understood, that nothing in the physical is absolute. It is all changeable down to the most minute particle and it all depends on the Meaning asserted by the Observer.

(16) John Hagelin, Ph.D., is a world-renowned quantum physicist, educator, public policy expert, and leading proponent of peace. Dr. Hagelin received his A.B. summa cum laude from Dartmouth College and his M.A. and Ph.D. from Harvard University, and conducted pioneering research at CERN (the European Center for Particle Physics) and SLAC (the Stanford Linear Accelerator Center). His scientific contributions in the fields of electroweak unification, grand unification, super-symmetry and cosmology include some of the most cited references in the physical sciences. He is also responsible for the development of a highly successful Grand Unified Field Theory based on the Superstring. Dr. Hagelin is therefore at the pinnacle of achievement among the elite cadre of physicists who have fulfilled Einstein's dream of a "theory of everything" through their mathematical formulation of the Unified Field-the most advanced scientific knowledge of our time. **L241**

Chapter 3

It is the one power that we have, our GOD Power, to assert Meanings to events and situations, and even to Matter itself, and cause them to change and re-form themselves according to our Meanings.

This idea of unlimited possibilities in Quantum Physics is the most important aspect of Reality. It is in the unlimited nature of Reality that one can create and elicit any combination of elements that he wants to create his own perfect Physical Life Experience.

C242 Meaning Is THE Primary Force of the Universe

Nothing is more Fundamental than Meaning. Every other Force and "Power" so to speak, is Manifested into existence from Meaning. It is Meaning that Creates, forms and sustains everything in the Universe in the first place, including Atoms and all of their parts.

In the last Video Example - Quantum Physics & Consciousness, John Hagelin, Ph. D. says that "We live in a World of Potential Electrons." That is to say that they are only Electrons when we expect them to be, otherwise they might not even exist.

All the "Forces" and "Energies" that we have come to believe were fundamental and a constant of Reality, are actually Manifested into existence. These include, Electricity, Magnetism, Gravity, Nuclear, etc. All of these are functions of Atoms and Matter which first has to be created by Meaning. Other creations such as Light, Time & Space, are also Manifested into existence as a result of Meaning.

"Classical Physics," has been used to explain and described these "Manifested Forces." However, later on in this book, we will be covering Example after Example where Fire doesn't Burn, Bullets don't penetrate flesh and finger tips can "See" like eyes. If these Forces were truly fundamental and primary, then they could not be violated and proven impotent. However time and time again we will see that Meaning has "Overridden" them, which could only happen if Meaning was more fundamental and more Powerful than these so called "Forces of Nature."

Quantum Physics & Painting   C243

When a painter uses a "Palette," he can mix any of the colors that he has in any way that he wants to. If he has Red, Blue, and Yellow, what colors will he make? Quantum Physics tell us that he has an unlimited range of possibilities and that a specific event cannot be predicted. It comes down to a choice and it is always based on the "Observer/Creator," which is the one whose consciousness is creating the Meaning that will elicit a certain response from the Universe. (Make the choice)

Since every color in the Universe can be created from these three colors it is impossible for us to know what color will be chosen, and all we will ever know is that he can choose any color he wants to. No matter what anyone else has ever done, wants to do, might do, or even what he should do, none of that has any bearing on what he might decide and elicit from the situation this time.

Chapter 5

Isn't it amazing that there are an infinite number of possible colors that can be made from just those three colors? Just like there is an infinite number different songs that a 3 piece band could play if they learned them.

If three colors or just three band members can create an infinite number of possible outcomes, then what are the possible number of outcomes from a very complex "Problem?" It boggles the mind. It might be said to be (Infinite x Infinite) and according to Quantum Physics, not a single one of those outcomes is certain. Every single one is possible depending on the "Observer" or the one who is asserting the Meaning to it.

Once the painter selects a certain amount of paint from each color and starts mixing them together he has given it Meaning and it will become a certain color. A certain amount of Red paint which is now the Meaning of the "Red Influence," immediately limits the possible outcomes. Once a certain amount of Blue Paint has been selected, then the Meaning of "Blue's Influence" has then been established and the possibilities are limited even further. Once the amount of Yellow has been selected, finally, it can now be only one certain outcome after that. Even though it is not mixed together yet, the Meanings that have been established are vibrating together in a combination that will elicit a certain color from the field of all possibilities.

However, even if and when the color is completely mixed together, it is still never "set in stone." That is no situation, no matter how final it seems, is ever really final. Just as he raises his brush to paint the new color on the canvas, he might decide to add more red or blue or even more yellow. Even if he has painted the new color on the canvas and it has dried and been there for years, he could come back and paint a new color over the old one. Nothing is ever final and unchangeable. It always remains a "Sea of Possibilities."

Quantum Physics relates to this level where the Meanings have not yet been established. That is why the "Observer/Creator" is so important and why nothing can be finalized. However, once the amounts of color have been selected, once the meanings have been chosen and established, then, and only then can "Classical Physics" take over and predict the exact outcome, the exact color that will result (For the Moment).

Every situation and event is composed of unlimited elements. It could be the whether the economy, the people involved, the time of day, the country in which it happens, the previous events, the future ramifications, and on and on it goes. Every single "Element" has an unlimited number of possibilities. That is, the outcome is not certain.

Let's look at the weather. It could be raining. Maybe that is a good thing or maybe not. But remember, no matter what the desired result is, every element has a possible Meaning available that will support that outcome. If each element can have unlimited Meanings in this given situation, then how many outcomes are possible with all of those possibilities combined? (Infinite x Infinite x Infinite etc.) In short, you can elicit any outcome that you want from any situation. It is Possible.

A244   P007

Note in this Illustration that the "Elements are Neutral" and have no fixed Meanings. They can either be good or bad elements depending on what you "Elicit" from them. In Quantum Physics, we know that nothing can be predicted for sure until the "Observer" is taken into consideration, because it is the "Observer/Creator" who will dictate the outcome by giving Meaning to the event. In any given situation, you can name at least 3 or 4 Good benefits and at least the same amount of Bad consequences for any "Element" in the situation. Can you imagine the infinite number of other Good and Bad aspects of that element that the Universe can produce that you haven't even though of? No matter what the "Element" is, it will become a Good thing or a Bad thing depending on what you are "eliciting" from the situation.

Chapter 3

A245

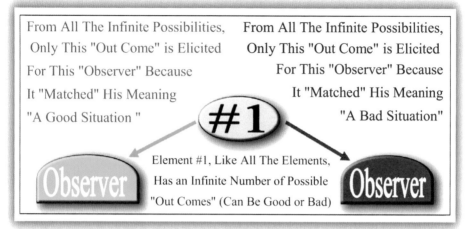

From All The Infinite Possibilities, Only This "Out Come" is Elicited For This "Observer" Because It "Matched" His Meaning "A Good Situation"

From All The Infinite Possibilities, Only This "Out Come" is Elicited For This "Observer" Because It "Matched" His Meaning "A Bad Situation"

Observer

Observer

Element #1, Like All The Elements, Has an Infinite Number of Possible "Out Comes" (Can Be Good or Bad)

When you are thinking that "Things are working out for me," then you are eliciting "good" aspects from the "Elements" of the situation. While there may be an "Infinite" number of possible benefits from "Element #1," the one that you will elicit will be the one that works perfectly with the "elicited" results from the rest of the "Elements." All of the exact responses will be elicited such that they interact with each other to perfectly create the overall result, whether it will be Good or Bad.

Not only does each "Element" add an infinite number of possible aspects or Meanings to the situation, but they also range from extremely bad to extremely good. This means that depending on the power of your emotional feeling on the matter, it will dictate the degree of Good Response or Bad Response that you elicit.

If you have great Fear and worry about the situation, you will elicit the very worst possibilities from all the "Elements" of the situation such that the overall result will be very bad. However, if you have great expectations and feel ecstatic about the situation, you will elicit the very best combinations of the elements possible.

When Things "Go Wrong" in Order to "Go Right" C246

This is where you have to understand that sometimes, the very best outcome for you might be a result that you don't recognize as a good one, but it still is. Just have faith that if you are always expecting the best, you will always get the best even if it doesn't look like it's "the best" at the time. You can't know all the things that are working for you at the higher levels of creation that "Know All" like the Universe. You may end up breaking up with your spouse and feel that was the worst outcome, just to find later that the new person you meet will be the Love of your Life forever. You can't know everything in advance.

You could be having the greatest day of your life. You wake up in a great mood and everything just seems to be working out. On the way to work, every traffic light turns green just in time. Your day couldn't get any better when you suddenly get hit by another car which totals yours and it is such a big mess that you have to miss work that day. Now what? First, consider that everything is working out for you, so this must be part of the "Best for you" plan in some way. However, in this case you find out later that the World Trade Center just got hit by a plane and it was right on your floor where you would have been sitting. While it was nice to find out later that the guy who slammed your car saved your life, you won't always know the direct benefit of circumstances that "seemingly went wrong." It's a gift when you do. Just remember, that even though things look like they are going wrong, they may be actually going the best way possible for you and you would have seen it, if you could have seen the "big picture."

Imagine that you are going west from New York to California. You think, naturally so, that the best way to go is straight, directly to California. As you are driving you notice that the road suddenly turns directly North.

Chapter 5

"What is the problem? You think. "I want to go West, not North." However, if you could go up in a helicopter and see the "Big Picture" you would realize that there was a huge body of water that the road was going around. If you had still gone straight, you would have gotten wet. Sometimes we have to go in unexpected directions, but we are still heading in the right direction over all.

What if the road is under construction and you have to take a long detour in the North direction? You might think, "There is no good reason for this, they should have made arrangements to still be able to go straight even if it was only one lane." This is of course a negative Meaning on an event, like any and every other event, that has no good or bad meaning to start with. However, since you have now given it the Meaning of "Bad," then according to Quantum Physics, the Observer has now given Meaning to the event, making a choice, and now the outcome can be predicted. As you expect, it is a long and slow detour with no redeeming benefits.

What if you took the approach that even thought the circumstances have changed and now seem more difficult, things are still always working out for you? Perhaps, as you took the detour, you passed a store that you would never have seen. It catches your attention (Resonating with you) and so you stop and check it out. It has the thing you have been looking for, for years, or while in the store, you meet someone who turns out to be the love of your Life, or who knows what else could happen. All of this wouldn't have happened if there had been no detour. Thank God for the Detour now.

When you were upset about the detour, you had passed that same store, but it did not catch your attention. How could it? It was one of the possible outcomes that would have been great for you, but you were only eliciting negative outcomes when you passed the store and so you passed right by. However, you did stop at another store that just sort of seemed like the place to stop for gas. But as you pulled in, you ran over a nail which flatted your tire and when you were waiting in line, someone pick pocketed you and now you have no money. Why did you stop there? It just seemed like the place to stop. Nothing just seems like the thing to do on its own. It is a function of Resonance. It caught your attention because you were eliciting negative outcomes, and that gas station had a few waiting for you.

So How Can You Know In Advance If An Unfortunate

Event Will End Up Being a Fortunate Event?

That is so Simple to answer and understand. Just look at your reaction to the situation and the Meaning that you give it. If you give it a Bad Meaning, it will not only turn out to be truly unfortunate, but, by the laws of Quantum Physics, you, the Observer, will have selected the outcome from the field of all possible outcomes by giving it a Bad Meaning and it will become even worse. However, if you give Positive Meanings to even the seemingly most unfortunate looking events and circumstances, you will cause them to become fortunate for you in some unexpected way.

It is most important for you to realize that none of this is a punishment for poor thinking or a reward for good thinking. It is only an attracting of more of what you are thinking, whether it is good or bad. Those "Seemingly Negative" things that happened to you might have been Positive things for someone else. So nothing is good or bad in itself. It is only a negative or a positive thing if you say so. If you label events as Negative, then you will get more of what you think is negative. If you label things and events as Positive you will get more things that you think are positive. You are the Observer, who dictates the specific outcome from the infinite number that is possible, by giving them Meaning.

The Party of Dice   C247

Imagine that you have been invited to a special party with all kinds of people there. It sounds great and you attend. Now imagine that people's personalities can be classified as a number from 1 to 10, with 1 being the worst and 10 being perfect and wonderful. As you walk into the party a weird magical thing happens. You and everyone else at the party turn into dice with 10 sides each, which is 4 more sides that the regular die, but matches our personality scale perfectly.

Chapter 5

145

Most people have many different personalities, depending on what the situation is. If it is a great situation they are at their best, but if it's not, they might turn into real jerks. This is like our guitar example. You can play a high note or a low note on the same guitar; it just depends on the situation.

Suppose that as you enter the party, you are feeling like a "4" because you had a hard day at work and whatever other excuse you can think of. As you go through the party as a vibration of "4", what do you think you will see? Will you see a "10?" Nope. Will you see a "1?" Nope.

Why not? Because as you radiate a vibration of a "4," you automatically elicit a vibration of "4," from everyone else, by the power of the universal matchmaker, "Resonance." Like a guitar, situations, circumstances, people and personalities, all have frequencies. If you were vibrating on the #4 string of a guitar the other guitars would respond by vibrating on their #4 string. If they didn't have a #4 string, you wouldn't even notice them. You can only notice those people who catch your attention. The people who catch your attention are those who are most like you and resonate in your presence and catch your notice. They think like you and talk like you. If they don't, you will soon move on to another conversation with other people who do.

Note that all this resonating and the like is happening at a level that you are not conscious. You think that you just happened to meet someone. But, No, you did not. Nothing in the Universe just happens by accident. Just so you can get this clear in your mind, think about the guitar store again. You are playing a #3 string, and all the other guitars that can and do resonate on the #3 note light up and catch your attention. Now, tell me how another guitar that does not have the ability to resonate on the third string can "Accidentally" turn on its light indicating resonance? It is impossible. Nothing responds by accident. It cannot. While it may look like it from your view point, in the Universal Reality, there is a reason and it's Resonance.

Back to the dice party. As you go through the party you will only see those who are like your "4." If they have no "4" ability, and cannot respond as a "4," they will have left the room before you got there, or they will be completely invisible to you. Someone will say to you "Did you see Bill?" And you will say "NO. Was he even there?" They will respond, "He was there all night and even sang on the Karaoke machine. I'm surprised that you didn't see him." (Obviously, he wasn't a "4," or you would have notice him.)

You go outside to collect your thoughts and actually get feeling better about yourself and suddenly you move up to an "8!" Wow! What a comeback. As you come back into the party and you look around, everything just seems better. The food tastes better, the atmosphere is better, the music is better, and even the people are all "8" and wonderful to talk to. You are eliciting a better result from everything in your environment. Even the same exact food that you didn't care for before, now taste great! Of course, some of the people that you were talking to earlier as a "4," are nowhere to be seen, because they can't be an "8" right now and so you can't see them anywhere.

However, you do see a person that you were talking to as a "4," and surprisingly, they are an "8" now just like you. As you start to talk to him he tells you, "I actually like you better right now, because earlier you seemed like a real jerk, but, now, I can see that you are a great person after all." And you remark "I felt the same way about you. I see now that you are great also." How can this be? This is because when you first saw him, you were a "4" and you elicited and brought out the "4" in him. So you both could only see the "4" in each other, even though, like a guitar, you had many other and better strings, the only one you both noticed in the moment, was the "4."

As you change your attitude and resonant Vibrational place, you will elicit different outcomes, meet different people, have different opportunities, because they are no longer invisible to you, but, instead, actually catch your attention and you catch their attention.

While this is the basic concept of how this works, it is not strictly based on personality alone. You may be repulsed by their personality, but be attracted to what they are talking about or the clothes they are wearing. We are very complex beings, there are a million ways that one person may Resonate with another. Even posture causes a resonate quality. Remember the Waitress example where she caused Resonance by saying the same exact words, and the computer agent who established Resonance by using the same head movements.

Objects made of the same metal, and even the same exact amount of metal, will have a different resonant quality based on the shape and form of the object. It is easy to notice the different resonant frequencies of objects as the frequency can be heard as a sound. If you tap on two glasses that are the same but have with different amount of water in them, they will sound different. If you have different size glasses or different size pots and pans, they all sound different. Like the bridge

Chapter 5

that ripped itself apart, all forms have an overall resonant value (Frequency). When you combine all of the aspects of the materials that they are made of etc, it all adds up to an overall resonant frequency for that object. That form aspect of resonance is the same for people.

Everything about a person adds up to their signature frequency. In a song, you can have 1 Guitar, 1 drum set and 1 singer, and still you can have billions and billions of different songs with their own unique frequency. Just imagine if you start adding in more guitars and horns and other instruments and more singers. People can be similar in some ways, while completely different in others. Still using our song metaphor, one person's "Horn Sound" may be a very similar frequency with another person's horn sound, and yet everything else is different. But, in that way, they resonate with each other. Maybe that sameness is that they both like dogs or cats, have the same hobby, or went to the same school.

When "Likeness" is perceived, it causes resonance. In psychology this is called "Mirroring" or mimicking. When one person makes the same gestures or takes on the same posture or talks in the same way as another, it causes "Likeness" and causes an almost automatic Rapport [17] between the two people.

We saw two examples of this in the Video Examples on the Waitress who got better tips, and the Computerized agent who got better agreement. It's not surprising, because "Likeness" is the basis of Resonance and Resonance has the ability to elicit an automatic response from the other object that it is in resonance with. Rapport could be thought of as simply, a high state of Resonance. So, if a Salesman creates "likeness," and therefore resonance with his customer, it is much easier for him to elicit a purchase from that customer. It is much easier to elicit agreement and action, from someone that you are in "Rapport" or Resonance, with.

---

(17) Rapport is one of the most important features or characteristics of unconscious human interaction. It is commonality of perspective: being "in sync" with, or being "on the same wavelength" as the person with whom you are talking. **L248**

The Smorgasbord Technique (For Attraction) C250

Life is like a Smorgasbord. It has everything that you could think of and then some. All you have to do is select what you want from the abundant variety that is life and forget the rest. The only thing is that this Smorgasbord is set up a little different than the normal one. In this one, you wander around the restaurant and look at what everyone else is eating. You are looking out at life around you in order to see what is available. I don't mean who or what specifically, but instead, the "elements" or pieces and parts that will make up your perfect meal or life experience. On a smorgasbord, you don't have meals that are already "put together," instead you only have the parts that make up the perfect Meal. You notice that one person has the main course that you really love, Roast Beef, and they seem to be enjoying it, so you make a mental note of it. Next, over there is another person who has the vegetable side dish, that you have always liked, corn, and so you make note of it. Then another has the bread that you want, but everything else they have you don't care for, but, that's O.K., because you are only looking at the bread anyway, just the part that you want. Finally, another person has the drink and the dessert that you like, Tea and Pecan Pie.

While life is like the Smorgasbord, in that you look for the different kinds of things and parts that you like, it is unlike the smorgasbord, because you can't actually get the separate individual parts and assemble the perfect experience. You cannot get a hand full of blond hair, and get a personality, then pick up the perfect body, and the face that you want and put it all together to create and assemble your perfect Mate. In life, you get "Package Deals" that are already

Chapter 3

assembled and ready to go. The smorgasbord technique was only to get in mind the elements that you wanted, now it's time to find the right package that already has those elements that you have "Pre-Selected." Let's work through an example to see how this works.

Let's say that You are looking for the perfect mate. How do you find the one that you want? Just like a Smorgasbord, you have to choose the traits that you want and give thought to them. If you want someone with blond hair, and you have given it some thought, all the people who have blond hair begin to resonate with you and catch your attention. Of course that is easy to understand because that is a "visual" thing, something that you can actually see. But the same holds true for anything or any aspect that you are looking for. You can "select" for a great personality. Then people with great personalities, begin to catch your attention even if they aren't saying a thing. Who they are is resonating with you at a psychic level that you cannot see but, still catches your notice. So now, that you have established two traits, those people who have Blond hair and a great personality have twice the resonant quality and catch your attention and stand out more than the ones with only blond hair or only a great personality. As you build your plate in more and more detail, the greater and greater the resonant quality and power becomes.

Now, you might have a situation where you notice someone in the park who is having a blast playing with their kids. They are having a great time and you think well I can see that they are married and so I can't have that. Wrong! STOP! Remember, this is a Smorgasbord situation. So you have noticed an item that is on someone else's plate already. So what? You are only collecting traits that you are interested in so that you can clearly have in mind what you want for yourself. As you build a more and more detailed idea of who this person is, they will stand out from the crowd, notice you and be noticed by you. You will notice each other. So, NOTICE how they play with their Kids and enjoy that personal trait that you like.

If you notice a trait that you like and then say I can't have them because they are married, or are a celebrity or are too old or too young or whatever, what you end up saying in a Vibrational way is that you can't have that trait! Maybe that person you are admiring in a movie is even dead, so what. You are only noticing things that you like in a person, that's all. So, instead, observe and really enjoy the trait that you love. See it in action. Get your fill of it. Get it clearly in your mind. As your trait list becomes more focused, the power of resonance becomes stronger and stronger, until one day, you bump into someone who is exactly who you have been looking for and it's love at first sight. It happens every day. By the way, this person was also thinking of someone like you, otherwise they would never have noticed you. Resonance is the Best Matchmaker in the Universe. Use it. It's free.

The Smorgasbord strategy works on anything and everything that you are wanting from a great job, to a new car or a new house, or to the Love of your life. All you have to do is look for examples of different aspects of what you want. Observe them and give great thought to them. As you add more and more detail to exactly what you want, its resonant power becomes greater and greater until the day arrives when everything magically falls into place. The last, but most important point is that you must really believe that you can have the thing that you want. Don't worry if you don't at first. The Universe has a wonderful way, of giving you more and more belief, as you become clearer about it. There will come a point where you will not only know that you can have it, but there will be no doubt that you will have it.

There is also the bad use of the Smorgasbord strategy. This is when you constantly give notice to and point out the things you don't want or don't like. You could say "I don't like Brunet colored hair," which would only cause you to notice everyone who has it. Then as you add the things that you don't want, the more and more frustrated you become because that's all you notice is the things that you don't like. Besides, it is much easier to think of what you do want than to name every single other thing that you don't want. That would be like naming thousands of colors that you don't want to paint your house, in order to have the only color left that is what you do want. Wouldn't it be easier to just name the one color that you do want and then just look for that one?

C251   The Catalog Store

Have you ever shopped in a catalog store where there was only one item on the shelf so you could look at it, but, you had to make a list of what you wanted and the store people would get it from the warehouse for you? When you got to the cash register, it would be on the conveyor belt waiting for you. There are still a few of these types of stores around. It is a good metaphor for how the Universe brings you what you think about.

Imagine that you have entered this store and you have a helper, the Universe, who is recording your order as you go along. Right away, you pass many items without even so much as a glance. They were of no interest to you and you paid no attention to them. Obviously, if you gave them no thought, then they are not in your mind and have no resonant power at all. Perfect! Then you come upon an item of interest. You pick it up and look at it closely. You check the price and read the directions and after a few minutes, you hear the Universe on the loud speaker say, "Select Item Number 32." You think what? I haven't decided yet. But you spent so much time examining it, that you now have a strong mental impression of it that now has a resonant power. You will now notice it in your World. What you notice becomes part of your World and experience.

So you say that's O.K. because I actually do like it and do want it. You move on. You casually notice a few more items, but quickly move on as soon as you realize that it is not something you want to notice in your World. You stop and spend enough time to select another item that you want and the Universe calls out to the cashier, "Place item number 58 on the conveyor belt for this customer." That's perfect because you wanted the item. Then out of the blue you notice that there is a pile of dog poop in the middle of the isle. You comment out loud "How did this get here?" You continue "This is a terrible thing and someone has to be held responsible for this! Where is the manager, I want to complain. They must have guard dogs in here at night and one of them made this awful mess." Suddenly, the Universe calls out "Place one pile of dog poop on the conveyor belt for this customer."

You cry out to the Universe "No you are misunderstanding me. I am only trying to make someone responsible for this. I don't want any myself!" And the Universe replies "You must have great interest in it, because of how much time and thought you are giving it. Anything that is so important to you that you would spend your precious time and thought on it, must be important enough to bring into your World. You have given enough thought to this that it now has a strong resonant power and you will notice piles of dog poop everywhere. You may even inadvertently step in some. It will show up in all the wrong places at the wrong time because that is exactly the vibration and thought you now have. That is what you will now notice."

At this point it is better to move on and forget about the whole thing, because if you continue to talk about it and complain, the Universe is going to order another helping of Dog Poop for you and you will notice even more of it. Nothing good can come from arguing and complaining about something, because it will only bring more of it to your door step. It may not be the exact same thing, but it will be the exact same problem for you.

The Universe has no ability to decide what you want and what you don't want, what is good for you and what is not. Instead it only uses its wonderful Matchmaker, "Resonance," to elicit what you think about. So, what you think about, you will notice more and more of. If you don't want it, don't think about it. Why would you spend even a minute of your short life paying attention to, and thinking about something that you don't like or want?

The Universe has no capacity, ability, nor does it have the desire to judge you. It only has the ability to bring into your experience those things that you think about, by the power of Resonance. They may be good or bad for you. Only you know if they are by the way your thoughts feel as you are thinking them.

C252   Your Thoughts Are The Invitation

If you are thinking about criminals all the time, it is likely that you will attract one into your experience. As you think about them, you begin to resonate with the criminal types. You bump into them on the street; you ask them for the time, you invite them to your home. However, all along you feel a connection to them because you are resonating with them. But, the connection is not friendship like you think, it's because they are the embodiment of the thoughts you have been thinking. As you resonate, you notice them, and they notice you. This of course is not a good thing for you (in this example). However, if you reviewed you thinking, you would remember that as you were giving thought to the criminal types, you weren't enjoying it much. That would be your clue that you are thinking about something that you don't want to attract into your experience.

The Universe has no judgment as to whether it would be good or bad for you to come in contact with a criminal. You see that in itself isn't good or bad. That is a personal judgment. While it may be bad for you, for a Policeman, it would be good to notice the criminal types. It's his job to find them, and so he gives great thought to them all the time hoping to attract them into his experience.

Same Likeness			**A253 P019**
Thought Meaning	+	Thought Meaning	= Physical Result & Meaning
This Person's Normal Thoughts & Beliefs Have Certain Frequencies **"I Might Get Robbed"**		Robber with Similar Frequency Thoughts **"I Want To Rob Someone"**	Resonance Activated Response Elicited **Robber Notices You & Your House**
Harmful Meanings Have Been Activated & Are Being Elicited From The Situation			

The Green Tuning Fork Vibrations are Good Meanings and they Resonate & Elicit ALL the things that will match them The Red Tuning Fork Vibrations are Bad Meanings and they Resonate & Elicit ALL the things that will match them

The Experience's of "Others"   C254
Always Becomes Re-Coded to Mean You

Your Vibrational system does not discriminate between what happens to others and what you want for yourself. You could be watching a news story on TV about someone else that has been robbed, or you could be driving by a severe accident on the highway, and even though you see it and perceive it as "happening to someone else," your vibration system recodes it as if it were you. This is because it is not WHO is involved, it is WHAT the subject matter is. So someone else in a car accident = you attracting it for yourself. Someone else on TV who has been robbed or gotten a disease = You having the same experiences for yourself.

Everything in your World only relates to you. You are the only one in the Universe that matters to you. So it doesn't matter what you see and who it is actually happening to, it will always be transformed into a future story about you, good or bad.

Nothing is ever good or bad by itself, so it is the same with this. This could be a good thing if you are watching a movie or hearing a story about someone getting rich, becoming successful or finding Love. The Universe will place you in the Role of the one who is succeeding or finding love and you will begin to attract that unto you. By all means, seek out those kinds of experiences for yourself. Get the feeling of the moment and not only enjoy the story line, but imagine it happening to you as well.

Chapter 5

C249   Your Head Above the Clouds

If you were able to stick you head above the clouds, you would no longer be able to see anything else below you. However, if there were other people with their heads above the clouds also, you all would be able to notice and see each other. If one of these other people had a great opportunity available, to whom could he offer it? He couldn't offer it to the people below him, because he can't see them and has no idea who they are. He can only offer it to the people with whom he is aware. That includes you. You see, when you are operating within a certain frequency range, you are only aware of those other people and circumstances that are within that range. Every other situation and person in the World may as well be invisible, because in reality, they really are.

That is why people promoting success always say, "Go to the Neighborhoods where you want to live. Hang out with the people that you want to emulate. Think like they do and you will see the same opportunities that they see." If instead you go the same places and think the same things that you have always done, you will always notice the same things that you have always noticed, and you will always have exactly the same opportunities that you had before.

Resonance Happens at the "Energy Level"   C255

Resonance is not just a visual thing, but instead happens at the "Energy" level where all real information is. That is where Consciousness is and where the actual Resonating happens. Because of this, Resonance can and does occur as a result of "Thoughts" which have no physical form, but which do have Meaning, and since it is always the "Meaning" that creates the Frequency that is in "Resonance," it could be said that it is the Meaning that is Resonating.

In the next Video Example(s), a dog picks up on the "Meaning" that his beloved owner is coming home. Pay very close attention to this example, because we will be referring to it throughout the rest of this book.

Video Example   V256

Dog Knows His Owner Is On the Way Home

V256   Video Example

Dog Knows His Owner Is On the Way Home (2)

What is this video about?

In this Video Example we will meet Rupert Sheldrake [18] who is a researcher that has been studying psychic phenomenon for many years. In this video Example, he is conducting a study on "Dogs That Know When Their Owners Are Coming Home." [19] It seems to be a common experience that dogs and cats, seem to sense and know right when their owners are coming home.

In order to eliminate all other possible explanations, he has carefully set up an experiment that will eliminate all possible explanations except a psychic communication. First, he figures out what might have caused the reaction, such as hearing the car approaching or even recognizing the sound of the owner's car. Or it could have been due to a normal time that the owner comes home. Or it could be someone in the house tipping off the dog that his owner is coming home. Finally, there is the question of exactly when the dog becomes aware that his owner is coming home.

First he has selected a random time in which the owner will come home, that is determined by the roll of the dice. Only the owner knows this time and no one else in the house does. That eliminates the usual time possibility, and the possibility of the dog being influenced by the people in the home. Then he has the owner come home in a taxi, which eliminates the possibility of the dog recognizing the sound of the owner's car. He then sets up a video camera in the home that watches the dog and another video camera that follows the owner throughout her day.

(18) Rupert Sheldrake, one of the world's most innovative biologists and writers is best known for his theory of morphic fields and morphic resonance, which leads to a vision of a living, developing universe with its own inherent memory. Rupert Sheldrake is a biologist and author of more than 80 scientific papers and ten books. A former Research Fellow of the Royal Soc)iety, he studied natural sciences at Cambridge University, where he was a Scholar of Clare College, took a double first class honours degree and was awarded the University Botany Prize. He then studied philosophy at Harvard University, where he was a Frank Knox Fellow, before returning to Cambridge, where he took a Ph.D. in biochemistry. He was a Fellow of Clare College, Cambridge, where he was Director of Studies in biochemistry and cell biology. As the Rosenheim Research Fellow of the Royal Society, he carried out research on the development of plants and the ageing of cells in the Department of Biochemistry at Cambridge University. **L259**

(19) Dogs that Know When Their Owners are Coming Home: and other unexplained powers of animals, New York, NY: Crown, 1999.

Book Review: #MoreReview The rich collection of dog tales and animal stories in this remarkable book makes it an appealing volume for dog lovers and anyone interested in animal behavior. It can be read at a much deeper level as well, but the book is very much worth reading for the animal episodes alone. There's the story of Jaytee, a mixed-breed terrier living in Northern England who correctly anticipated the return of his owner Pam 85 percent of the time during a year-long experiment. Pam kept a log of her own travels including the varying and random times when she set off for home. Her parents kept a log of Jaytee's activities including when he went to the French door to await his mistress. The match-up was remarkable. There's the tale of a cat named Sami living in Washington, D.C., who waits by the door about 10 minutes before either his owner Jeanne or her boyfriend arrives home at Jeanne's high-rise apartment at widely varying and unexpected times. How did Sami or Jaytee or the other critters in the book know their owners had set out for home and would soon arrive -- when the people at home did not know? Stories of horses, monkeys, birds and other species are included in the book as well. Their "unexplained powers" range from anticipating their owners' arrival to coming to an owner's rescue from a considerable distance to expressing grief when a parent or offspring dies, again from a far distant place. Also considered are such phenomena as homing abilities and the coordinated behavior of groups of animals, birds and fish ISBN 0-609-60092-3. **L260**

Chapter 5

The video cameras each have a synchronized clock that shows the exact time on the video. This way you can watch both videos side by side and see exactly what is happening with the owner and the dog at the same exact moment.

The owner's activities for the day included some shopping with a friend and eating at a restaurant. After their meal, they leave the restaurant, and have a little conversation outside. The owner decides it's time to head home and waves a taxi over to pick them up. AT THAT VERY MOMENT, the dog that had been sleeping picks up his head and his ears stand up. He looks around and gets up and heads to the door. It takes the owner a while to get home, because she was far away to start with. When she arrives the dog is at the door as usual and wagging his tail in great excitement to see his owner home again. It is a beautiful scene.

Rupert also tells a story about cats. It seems that cats are particularly bothered at the notion of going to the Vet. He has conducted surveys by the owners of cats as well as the vet clinics and has found a correlation between an owner thinking about taking the cat to the vet and then coming home to find the cat is hiding somewhere and can't be found.

It doesn't matter if the owner is home when he thinks about it or at his office, his thoughts are received by the cat and the cat hides. This seems to be well known by the vets because they don't even set appointments for cats any more. They just go by the time the owner actually gets his cat there.

What does this example show and what does it mean?

This video example shows that a dog can sense when his owner is coming home. Not when the owner is near the home, but exactly when the owner decides to come home. It is at the moment of decision. The dog responds the moment that there is the Meaning "My owner will be here soon," because he is able to receive and understand that meaning.

This is a Resonant Situation of like Frequencies. The Dog is thinking I am waiting for my "Owner to Come Home," and when the Owner thinks "I'm going Home" that is a Match. The dog feels the resonant quality and is able to subconsciously or even perhaps consciously, recognize that his owner is on the way home. Just in the same way as hearing the phone ring means someone is calling or the doorbell means that someone is at the door.

There are several important points here. **Number one.** Meaning has a Frequency that permeates the Universe, and Resonates with those situations, circumstances, people, and even dogs, that are like that frequency or to which that frequency is relevant. The important thing here is, that millions of dogs had no awareness that this owner was going to her own home. It wasn't relevant to them. It did not resonate with them, it had no meaning to them and as a result it was invisible to them.

Important point number two is that the meaning that was sent when the owner decided to go home wasn't a special event. She didn't make an effort to "Send a message to her dog," but instead it was just the casual, normal, everyday experience of making a decision. It was a very small slice of experience. The facts are that when the owner was shopping and decided that she liked a certain item, that meaning was transmitted to the Universe. When she ordered her lunch, that order was transmitted to the Universe. If she had noticed something that she liked or didn't like those meanings were transmitted to the Universe. Everything that you think and do is creating meaning that is radiating from you and being transmitted like a radio signal to the Universe and everything in it.

Even though every other animal, person, or situation in the Universe had the opportunity to hear and receive that Meaning, it was only relevant to this particular dog, and it was the only meaning that he noticed. He didn't notice when the owner ordered lunch. That wasn't relevant and had no meaning to him. When some other person decided to go home, that wasn't noticed by him either, because it wasn't his owner and so it had no meaning to him. The only vibration that he was "Tuned into" was the one that had the meaning "My owner is coming home to me." So, when that one specific vibration, from out of the trillions of vibrations being transmitted by billions of people, came across him, it caught his attention, and elicited a reaction from him. It was the only one that "Resonated with him."

The point is that you are like a radio station that is constantly broadcasting your meanings to the Universe. When those meanings meet a relevant person, situation or even a dog, there is a reaction and an elicited response.

That is why your GOD Power is so important. If you constantly adjust your meanings and vibrations that you are sending out to be exactly what you want, then Resonance will be working in your benefit, setting up situations for you, bringing people, places, circumstances and things to your attention and bringing you to their attention.

All Resonance is doing is matching up your meanings with the appropriate situations that will then be interacting with you at some point. Be sure that the situations that you are lining up for your self are good ones. In the case of the dog, the owner was lining up a hearty welcome from her beloved pet in the "Future" by a thought that she was having in her "Present"

However, Sheldrake also mentions in the Video example that people have a very hard time getting their cats to the vet. They try to call the vet from their work so that the cat doesn't know that it will be going to the vet, but still, when the owner gets home, the cat is nowhere to be found. The "Dreaded" meaning was received by the cat anyway, no matter when or where it was decided or transmitted by the owner.

Likewise if you are afraid that you will be robbed or bitten by a dog, you are transmitting that meaning to the Universe, and when the time is right, you will have a most unwelcomed homecoming. They say that dogs can smell fear, but they are only receiving the Meaning that "You expect them to bite you," and so they do because that is what you are eliciting from them.

Dog's Response — A257

Thought Meaning	+	Thought Meaning	=	Physical Result & Meaning
This Person's Normal Thoughts & Beliefs Have Certain Frequencies "I'M Coming Home"		Dog Has Certain Frequency Thoughts "I Want My Owner To Come Home"		Resonance Activated Response Elicited Dog Is Waiting Excitedly For Owner

The Dog Noticed The Green Vibrational Thought - His Owner Is Coming Home

(From All possible frequencies with all kinds of Meanings only one is Noticed and Activated)

Cat's Response — A258

Thought Meaning	+	Thought Meaning	=	Physical Result & Meaning
This Person's Normal Thoughts & Beliefs Have Certain Frequencies "I'M Taking The Cat To The Vet"		Cat Has Certain Frequency Thoughts "I Hate Going To The Vet"		Resonance Activated Response Elicited Cat Is Hiding in Panic, When The Owner Comes Home

The Cat Noticed The Red Vibrational Thought - A Trip To The Vet Is Comming

(From All possible frequencies with all kinds of Meanings only one is Noticed and Activated)

Chapter 5

C261 **Plant Uses Resonance to Read a Persons Thoughts**

If you think that example was wild, you will really enjoy this one. Cleve Backster, [20] is an expert in using polygraph equipment, [21] which detects differences in skin conductivity that are usually associated with lying, but, are actually as a result of "Arousal." He was just messing around one day when he made an incredible discovery that "Plants can read our Minds." The following is an account of his discovery as it happened, in his own words. In this account he was showing slides and pointing out aspects of them to the audience. I don't have the slides he was using and all I have here is the transcript of the presentation.

For whatever reason, it occurred to me that it would be interesting to see how long it took the water to get from the root area of this plant, all the way up this long trunk and out and down to the leaves. After doing a saturation watering of the plant, I thought, "Well gee whiz, I've got a lot of polygraph equipment around; let me hook the galvanic skin response section of the polygraph onto the leaf."

Now this is a whetstone bridge circuit that is designed to measure resistance changes, and I felt that as the contaminated water came up the trunk and down into the leaf that the leaf becoming more saturated and a better conductor it would give me the rising time of the water....I would be able to get that on the polygraph chart tracing.

Well this was the thing that started it. Now the thing trended downward rather than upward, which amazed me a little bit because it should have been going slowly upward on the tracings, if it was going to show a drop in resistance. I moved it up here - this was my move - and then it came down again, and this is the thing that amazed me right here because

(20) Cleve Backster (born 1924) is a polygraph expert best known for his controversial experiments with biocommunication in plant and animal cells using a polygraph machine in the 1960s which led to his theory of "primary perception." He is currently director of the Backster School of Lie Detection in San Diego, California. Backster began his career as an Interrogation Specialist with the CIA, and went on to become Chairman of the Research and Instrument Committee of the Academy for Scientific Interrogation. His course of study changed dramatically in the 1960s, when he claimed to have discovered that a polygraph instrument attached to a plant leaf registered a change in electrical resistance when the plant was harmed or even threatened with harm. He argued that plants perceived human intentions, and as Backster began to investigate further, he also claimed to have found that other human thoughts and emotions caused reactions in plants that could be recorded by a polygraph instrument. He termed the plants' sensitivity to thoughts "primary perception," and first published his findings from the experiments in the International Journal of Parapsychology The article was met with wide criticism of his research methods, however Backster gained the interest of other researchers, and he expanded his experimental range to test for primary perceptions in other life forms, such as yogurt, bacteria, and human cells His work was inspired by the research of Sir Jagadish Chandra Bose,who claimed to have discovered that playing certain kinds of music in the area where plants grew caused them to grow faster. **L264**

(21) Polygraph Machine. A polygraph (popularly referred to as a lie detector) is an instrument that measures and records several physiological responses such as blood pressure, pulse, respiration, breathing rhythms, body temperature and skin conductivity while the subject is asked and answers a series of questions, on the theory that false answers will produce distinctive measurements. The polygraph measures physiological changes caused by the sympathetic nervous system during questioning. Within the US federal government, a polygraph examination is also referred to as a psychophysiological detection of deception (PDD) examination. Polygraphs are in some countries used as an interrogation tool with criminal suspects or candidates for sensitive public or private sector employment. The use and effectiveness of the polygraph is controversial, with the manner of its use and its validity subject to ongoing criticism. **L265**

Chapter 3

this contour right away...I'm looking and thinking, "That's got the contour of a human being tested, reacting when you are asking a question that could get them in trouble."

So I forgot about the rising water time and said, Wow, this thing wants to show me people-like reactions. "What can I do that will be a threat to the well being of the plant," similar to the fact that a relevant question regarding a crime could be a threat to a person taking a polygraph test if they're lying.

About 15 minutes along - 13 minutes and 55 seconds along in this initial observation...I had tried different things to try to get a reaction from this plant - I had even dipped a neighboring leaf into a cup of rather warm coffee - and the plant didn't show me anything like a reaction. It showed me, if anything, boredom, and just continued to go downwards. If this thing were an individual, the fact that they were getting bored and sleepy. But over here, the idea occurred to me, the idea occurred to me - and only the idea - "I know what I am going to do: I am going to burn that plant leaf, that very leaf that's attached to the polygraph." Now I didn't have matches in the room. I wasn't touching the plant in any way. I was maybe five feet away from the desk. I was essentially away from the plant.

The only new thing that occurred was my intent to burn that plant leaf. Right here, split second-wise, was when I thought of burning that plant leaf and the image entered my mind. I wasn't using words at all. And up that the thing went into a wild agitation. Now this was very late at night and towards morning. The building was empty and there was just no other reason for this reaction. This had been going along at a fairly stable level all the way up to this point. So this amazed me. This, I would say, would be a very high quality observation, and my consciousness hasn't been the same since. And this happened in 1966. I thought, "Wow! This thing read my mind!" It was that obvious to me right then.

So then I went to get some matches from the next room. The secretary was a smoker, and I got some matches out of her desk and brought them in. The next will show where I came back in the room, right about here. I lit the match. I was even into burning a neighboring leaf rather than the leaf I had hooked up. Somehow that was already a special leaf. Even before I had a chance to do this I thought, "Well, this massive degree of reaction that I'm getting here, I wouldn't be able to see any additional reaction if it did occur."

So I thought, "Well, let me reverse the process and remove the threat from the room." So I took the matches back out of the room here, came back in at this point, and the thing just evened right out again, which really rounded it out and gave me a very, very high quality observation.

Now when my partner in the polygraph school we were running at the time came in, he was able to do the same thing also, as long as he intended to burn the plant leaf. If he pretended to burn the plant leaf, it wouldn't react.

Plant's Response To "Actual" Threat   A262

Thought Meaning	+	Thought Meaning	=	Physical Result & Meaning
This Person's		Plant Has Certain		Resonance Activated
Thoughts & Beliefs		Frequency "Thoughts"		Response Elicited
Have Certain		& Vibrations		**Plant Is Responding**
Frequencies		**"I Don't Want**		**In Panic, When The**
"I'M Going To Harm		**To Be Harmed"**		**Person Comes Over**
(Burn) That Plant"				

The Plant Noticed The Red Vibrational Meaning - Harm Is Comming

(From All possible frequencies with all kinds of Meanings only one is Noticed and Activated)

Plant's Response To "Pretend" Threat   A263

Thought Meaning	+	Thought Meaning	=	Physical Result & Meaning
This Person's Thoughts &		Plant Has Certain		**NO Likeness**
Beliefs Have Certain		Frequency "Thoughts"		**NO Resonance**
Frequencies		& Vibrations		**NO Response**
"I'M Going To Do		**"I Don't Want**		**Plant Does Not**
Nothing To That Plant"		**To Be Harmed"**		**Respond**

The Plant Noticed Nothing - No Vibrational Meaning Was Relevant

(From All possible frequencies with all kinds of Meanings NONE are Noticed and Activated)

Chapter 5

It could tell the difference between pretending you are going to, and you are actually doing it, which is quite interesting in itself from a plant psychology standpoint. [22]

Like the dog example above, the plant was aware of his "Meaning" in a nonphysical, psychic way. But, unlike the happy dog, the plant was very unhappy, because the plant was going to be the receiver of an unwelcomed event that was on its way.

Notice the second to the last paragraph where the plant only reacted to actual meaning to harm, and not to the "pretending to harm." This translates very well into Meaning. When he had the actual intention to harm the plant, that was an actual Meaning of "Harm is on its way," while, his effort to "pretend," had a Meaning of, "No Harm is on its way." As always, it is only the Meaning that is of any consequence. As you can deduce, the physical actions of intended harm and intended trickery, would be exactly the same. There would be movement towards the plant with a match in hand. This clearly demonstrates, that even with identical actions, it is only the actual Meaning that counts.

Additionally, like the dog example above, the experimenter, was always "Transmitting" his meaning out to the Universe, even when at first he had no idea that it was being received.

You are **ALWAYS TRANSMITTING** your Meanings out into the Universe, and those people, places, events, situations, things and yes, even plants, who resonate with the vibration of your Meaning, respond in their own way.

(22) Silva Method Research Primary Perception **L266**

Source: Primary Perception, Biocommunication with Plants, Living Foods, and Human Cells - the following is an excerpt of Cleve Backster's primary perceptions research and notes from a recent live presentation at a Sylva centre.

Video Example Plants Have Consciousness   V267

What is this video about?

This Video has many examples and demonstrations that have been performed and all prove that Plants have Consciousness. In the first segment, Backster himself recounts his first experience that plants can read his thoughts and respond. Just as he was explaining in the information you just read, (above), he had connected a polygraph machine to the leaf of a plant and was trying to get a reaction out of the plant without success. (A polygraph machine, is also called a "Lie Detector," and what it does is measure the change in the conductivity of the skin, or in this case the leaf. When there is a change in the conductivity, it is an indication of nervousness.) He suddenly thought of burning the plant's leaf, and at the exact moment that he had the thought and the intention of burning the leaf, the plant reacted wildly. He said "That moment in February 2, 1966, changed the rest of my life."

(Same Video As Above) (1:52) The Second demonstration on this Video is also of Backster trying a different test. He wanted to see if a Plant could and would react to the death of Brine Shrimp. He set up the experiment like before with the plant hooked up to the polygraph machine. In a room next door to the plant, he had live Brine Shrimp in a small cup suspended above a pot of hot boiling water. In order for him to be sure that there was no Human interaction in the experiment, he not only set up the experiment to work automatically by a random timing device, but, he also left the office and drove some distance away so that his presence wouldn't interfere with

Chapter 5

the results. At the random time, selected by the machine, the automatic device dumped the Brine Shrimp that were in a small white cup, into the boiling water, to their death. At that exact moment, as expected, the plant showed a reaction. This proved that the plant was sensitive, and "Felt" the death of the Brine Shrimp in the next room at the exact moment of their death.

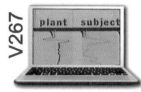

(Same Video As Above) (4:04) The Third Demonstration shows that a Plant is able to feel a person's emotional arousal. In this carefully set up experiment, the plant once again is attached to a polygraph type device and isolated in a plastic box to eliminate any possibility of interference in the experiment. Next, a person connected to the same type of equipment, is watching a provocative movie within a few feet of the plant. Right when a very sensual scene is shown on the movie screen, which causes the test subject to respond Emotionally, the plant responds also. The experiment shows that the plant was responding to the heightened emotional response of the person.

(Same Video As Above) (6:16) In this Forth demonstration, a woman tries to teach her plant the alphabet. It's not quite clear how its set up, but it appears that the plant is connected to a polygraph type device that is then connected to some sort of speaker. When she talks to the plant, it seems to respond in an audible way.

(Same Video As Above) (6:51) Segment Five is a demonstration from the Soviet Union. Once again, it seems that a cabbage plant is connected to a polygraph type device that is displayed on an electrical monitor with an audible response as well. This interesting demonstration shows that the cabbage plant reacts widely to a cabbage being chopped up in its presents.

The most interesting aspect of this experiment has two cabbage plants side by side with one that is connected to the monitoring device and one that is not. One by one, several lab assistants, each walk up to the plant that is not connected and stands for a moment and then exits the room. After several people have "Visited" the plant, one actually destroys it by ripping it apart with their bare hands and then exits the room. Naturally, and as you would expect by now, the other plant, the one connected to the monitoring equipment, reacts wildly to this.

But, the most interesting part of the experiment comes next. After some time passes and the plant has settled back down, the assistants each enter the room again. As each one enters, there is no reaction from the plant. But as soon as the actual person, who ripped apart the other plant, enters the room, the plant goes crazy again. The plant was able to recognize the guilty person who "killed" the other plant.

What does this example show and what does it mean?

This Video Example makes several great points. First, we are always sending out meaning. Every emotion that we feel, we send out to the Universe. However, even though it is "Heard and Received" by the entire Universe, it is only noticed by the people, places, situations, events, dogs, plants and whatever else that Resonates with its meaning.

You may be thinking that it's time for you to stop working with these plants and go home. You will find no reaction from the plant to this meaning. However, your dog will be delighted to receive this Meaning and reacts to it instantly by waiting for you at the door. The Meaning has no similarity to any Vibrational frequencies that the plant has. It has no idea that you were even thinking that, because it only knows what it notices, and it only notices what resonates with a vibration that it has. So, if you decide to try another experiment and think about burning the plant, the plant will go crazy, but your dog, will not notice.

The next point that I would like to make is in regard to the cabbage killing experiment. "How did the plant KNOW exactly who killed the other cabbage?" It is obvious that we all have our own individual "Vibrational Signature." That is to say that we are unique in every way including the Vibrational energy we are constantly emitting. Like our song example, even though the elements of the songs may be the same, such as the same instruments are played, but it is still easy to tell them apart when you listen to them. The instruments may be the same, but the song is different. We all are unique in every way and can be easily identified by that unique Vibrational signal.

Chapter 5

In the same way that the dog could tell that it was his owner that was coming home and not somebody else, so too this cabbage could tell exactly who the person was that killed the other cabbage by their unique Vibrational pattern.

This is the same unique "Vibrational Signature" that identifies us when we are resonating with our World. Every single person, place, thing, event, situation, dog or plant, knows that it is us specifically, when we are in Resonance together. How else could it work? We couldn't have Resonance be the "Universal Matchmaker," if it wasn't sure who sent the Vibrational signals, now could we?

The Cabbage plant received the signal of death, and the Vibrational signal identifier as to who was responsible. The cabbage plant's reaction when that same person returned to the room, wasn't from a need for revenge, (Thank God), it was from a place of fear and self protection. The plant knew it was possible that it was in danger also. This was very similar to Backster's original experiment with the match and his test plant.

Finally, the most important point that this Video Example makes is that Plants seem to have consciousness without a brain. If it were us, we would say that "we saw the danger with our eyes, and it sent a signal to our Brain, which sent out adrenalin to our muscles for the fight or flight syndrome." That's our realistic and rational way of explaining how Physical Reality works. But as we will see in the Chapter called "What is Reality?", nothing is actually going on physically. Everything that we see and feel is only a physical representation of a nonphysical creation.

Obviously, the plant has no brain, which we have always felt was the place where consciousness resides. But it does not. It is in the "Mind" (Not Brain) which resides in the energy realm. We will cover this more later on in the book. I just wanted to point it out while it's fresh in your mind. Consciousness is not a physical property. That means that the Brain which is a "physically oriented object" is not the place where consciousness resides.

The most important thing to realize about how this all works, is that you may never know who or what is Resonating with your Meanings. It could be the person of your dreams, that you have been giving much thought to, makes a wrong turn on the interstate, "Seemingly by accident," and ends up stopping at your store and meeting you as a result. Or, it could be a truck driver, who gets distracted for a moment, "Seemingly by accident," and pulls into your lane of traffic. Everything in the Universe is "Responding and Reacting," to the sum total of all the vibrations that it is Resonating with.

Maybe, you have been giving quite a bit of thought to exactly who you would like to meet, just like you are supposed to, but, you are also thinking, "Somebody else always seems to get the good ones." So the person who made the wrong turn, and ends up in your store, is in your sights just long enough for you to recognize that "They are the one," then someone else steps up and offers some help to them. Sure enough, they leave together. That could have been you, but just as you predicted, and created, it was not. It will never be "You," as long as you send out the meaning that it's never you.

Remember the Dog and the Plant, the next time you start thinking recklessly about things that you want. Every single thing you are thinking is flying across the Universe, faster than the speed of light, making all the right moves for you, or the wrong ones. It's your decision as to what that will be. The person or opportunity of your dreams could be excitedly waiting for you like the dog, or trying their best to avoid you like the cat. It all depends on what you have set up for yourself based on the Meanings that you are sending.

Chapter 3

C268   The Golden Rule

> *"Do Unto Others*
> *As You Would Have*
> *Them Do Unto You"*

Never have we fully understood how important the "Golden Rule" was than we do now. This principle has been known since early times. As powerful as it is, it doesn't limit any of your particular thoughts or acts. It just means don't do anything (or Think anything) about another that you wouldn't want done or thought about you. The genius of this is in its simplicity and scope. You see, this Golden Rule and "Karma," places the responsibility of your own actions and thoughts at your own feet **by your own judgment**. Anything that you think, say or do about or to another, creates a vibration that has a resonant quality. Whatever you are and are about, resonates with others who are the same way and it brings it back to your doorstep.

Some call this Karma. What you put out in the Universe, you get back. What you sow, you reap. When you are kind in thought and deed to others, **by your own measure**, you will find circumstances manifesting in your life in which you will be the beneficiary of good friends and good fortune. There is no escape from reaping what you sow. If you are able to "beat" others in business and succeed financially at the cost to another, you may suffer with bad health, or bad relationships. If you are inconsiderate of others, you will find that you will be on the receiving end of inconsideration, at the very least.

However, there is one saving grace for all of us. We are judged by our own measure. In other words, we judge ourselves. It makes no difference what others may think, so as long as you feel good about your own thoughts, words and deeds. If you feel good about yourself, you will reap an abundant life, full of joy and happiness, the joy & happiness that you have given to others. Before long you will be experiencing events, circumstances and friends who make you feel great about yourself and life.

Just Like Old Friends　　　　　C269

Have you ever met someone and it seemed like you have been good friends for years? And did you notice that you both felt the same way? How do you explain this? When you have been friends with someone for a very long time, you become more and more alike, which causes a strong Resonant effect, due to your growing likeness. The longer you know someone the more alike you become. As a result, you can actually feel the resonance between you. It's a feeling of Closeness (Likeness).

However, when you meet a new person that has many qualities that are just like you, you have a resonant feeling of likeness that feels like longtime friendships. The reason it feels like long time friendship, is because those are the only relationships that have that strong likeness and resonant quality. So when you meet someone new who has that same feeling, the only thing you can compare it to is a long term friendship. Often people who feel this strong resonant feeling will say "It feels like we have known each other for years." The reason is because it normally takes years to become that Resonantly alike.

Chapter 5

C270   The Music Is Everywhere and It's Nowhere

A radio is a great metaphor for understanding Frequencies and Resonance. In my seminars, I will have two radios one tuned to a station that plays great music and one tuned to a frequency that has no music. On stage I will tell the audience that I hear the music wherever I go. I turn on the radio that is tuned to a great radio station, and sure enough the music is playing. I run to the back corner of the auditorium and turn on my radio and again I hear the Music perfectly. I run to the other far corner of the auditorium and still I can hear the music. I come back to the stage and no matter where I go I can hear the music. So I announce to the audience that, "The music is everywhere."

My assistant comes on stage with the other radio and announces that he doesn't hear the music. I ask him "What are you going to do about it?" He replies "Well, I'm going to go to the back right corner of the auditorium where I'm going to get a new job, and then I'll be able to hear the music." I tell him "Give it a try." So he runs to the back right corner and announces that even though he changed his job, he still can't hear the music. Once again I ask "What are you going to do about it?" He replies "Well, I'm going to go to the back left corner of the auditorium where I'm going to get a new girlfriend, and then I'll be able to hear the music." I tell him "Give it a try." So he runs to the back left corner of the auditorium and announces that even though he got a new girlfriend, he still can't hear the music. Once again I ask "What are you going to do about it?" He replies "Well, I'm going to go back to the stage and move across the country to a new home, and then I'll be able to hear the music for sure." I tell him "Give it a try." He runs back to the stage again, and still, no music.

So, then I announce to the audience "The Music is everywhere and it's nowhere." When you can't hear the music, and you aren't happy where you ARE RIGHT NOW, you can't find happiness and hear the music by changing your job, finding a new girlfriend, or moving. In fact nothing you can do will bring you happiness. You have to first tune yourself to the happiness station where you are, and then you will notice happiness everywhere and no matter where you are, or what you do, you will hear the music and feel the happiness. Happiness is a state of mind that begets happy thoughts and attracts happy experiences. When you **Decide on Happiness**, you can see it in everything. It has a very powerful Resonant quality, that brings out, elicits, the happiness, the happy aspects, of any situation to the forefront, in perfect view where you can not only see and experience the happiness, but you can hear it's beautiful music, often in the form of laughter.

Chapter 5

You Can Have Everything That You Dream Of,

C272 *Unless You Want It!*

At first this sounds crazy. Isn't everything that you Dream of, by definition the things that you want? How is it that, "You can have everything that you dream about, but you can't have it if you want it?" Yes, of course I will explain.

We have learned up to this point that Meaning creates Frequency and that Frequency utilizes the Power of Resonance to elicit "its kind" from the Universe. So far, so good. However, it is at this point that we are going to need some "Fine Tuning" of our Understanding to get the most out of it all.

Once again, it is all about your GOD Power of assigning Meaning. You have to be sure that the Meaning that you are giving to the situation is the right one. I don't mean that in a way to say that anything is right or wrong, but, instead to say that it is the correct Meaning to use to get the result that you want. Obviously, if it elicits the wrong result, it was the wrong Meaning. When deciding on Meanings and the subtle differences in their eliciting power, just remember the title of this section because it will guide you perfectly every time.

"You Can Have Everything That You Dream Of, Unless You Want It."

First, let's start with the beginning of the phrase, "You can have everything that you Dream of." The key words in this segment are the words "Dream Of." When you Dream of something what is that like? If you are dreaming of a new sports car, aren't you driving it? Aren't you showing it off to others or enjoying it in some other way? When you are Dreaming about something, you are usually in the experience of "Having It." You are in the experience of "enjoying it now." Dreams are fun and always in the moment of the experience. If you had the Meaning of, "I have this now and I am enjoying it," then you will be eliciting the experience of, "I have this now and I'm enjoying it."

On the other hand, what is the feeling and experience of, "Wanting something?" Is it a joyful experience? Is it the Meaning of "I have this now," or is it the Meaning of, "I don't have this now and I am not enjoying it at all." Can you picture yourself looking in the showroom where the fancy sports cars are, both hands covering the sides of your face so that you can see better? The sports car is on the other side of a barrier that separates you from it. In the language of Meanings, a quarter inch of glass, might as well be a million miles, because it is not yours and you don't have it. The actual feeling might be described as "Anxious," or "Wanting," or "Needing," or maybe even "Desperation." So these feelings are the basis of your Meanings. You will elicit more "Wanting," "Anxiousness," "Needingness," and become even more "Desperate."

So you can clearly see the difference of the two Meanings. Have you ever Dreamed that you were at the window of the Sports Car dealership wanting the car? No, that has never happened. When you Dream of these wonderful things, you already have them and are enjoying them. That is the ideal place to create Meanings that elicit their kind from the Universe. Whenever you feel yourself "Wanting," just turn it into "Dreaming." That way you thoughts go from the anxiety of not having it, to joyous thoughts of experiencing it as if you already had it. This might be called "Day Dreaming."

Chapter 5

"Day Dreaming" is the most wonderful state of being for Manifesting. When you are Day Dreaming, you are immersed in your thoughts and your imagination is running wild with all the possibilities. Day Dream whenever you can, because when you Day Dream, your judgment is temporally suspended and all things are possible. When they are all possible, you are creating Meanings that will be eliciting and attracting things to you, so that one day, the impossible, will become your Reality.

Throughout this book I will be telling you to think about the things that you want. I haven't said to think about "Wanting them." I said to think about them. What color do you like? Where would you have it? What about it do you like or Love? There is a HUGE difference between thinking about something and "Wanting it."

Enjoy it in your mind as you build all of its elements, (Smorgasbord) but don't create thoughts and Meanings that it is over there and you are over here. In a Dream situation you are already experiencing everything that you want. There is no need to call it wanting or experience wanting, if you can experience Dreaming instead. Besides, if you are good at Dreaming of it, it can be almost as good as already having it. It is the next best thing to actually having it. But, no matter how good you are at wanting something, it is still no fun to experience the wanting of it.

The best point of view is of course to "Dream" about it. That is, think about it as if in a Dream. That is a Meaning of "Having" which will elicits and attracts "Having." The next Best is to think about it like you are planning on getting it or doing it. This has a Meaning of "Having Soon" which will elicits and attracts "Having Soon." But, whatever you do, don't want it and agonize over not having it, because that will make sure that you are always wanting it forever, nonstop. That will have a Meaning of "Don't Have" and you will elicit and attract circumstances and events that will keep you feeling that you "Don't Have."

The New Comers   A271 C271

The wise old man would sit at the train station and greet the new comers who would get off the train. They always asked him about his little town. They would say, "What is this town like?" He would always ask in return, "What is it like where you come from?"

 They would say that it was mean and nasty, nobody ever waved and no one cared about anyone else that is why they are moving to this new town. He would smile and then reply, "Well that's exactly what you will find here. You will find it's just the same everywhere."

Every now and again he would get a different answer to his question. Sometimes they would respond in a very positive way.

 "It's wonderful where we come from. Everybody smiles and tries to help each other, it was a wonderful town. We sure hated to leave it." "Well," he would say, "It's your lucky day. This town is just the same as you described your town to be. Everyone is nice and wants to help each other. It is a wonderful place to live."

The wise old man knew, that it was the Resonant quality of the New Comers, that created their experiences. Whatever their state of mind was and whatever they expected to see and find, is just what they would find. It didn't matter what town they would go to, it would always be the same as the town they had left. Whatever they were about themselves would elicit the same from the people they came in contact with, and they would eventually find their own kind. Resonance has a way of sorting things out and getting the people who belong together, to meet and get together. That is the natural and perfect function of Resonance, the "Universal Matchmaker."

Chapter 5

C273   "911" – A Case Study in Resonance

The events of September 11, 2001 are horrible and unfortunately, will always be remembered. I say unfortunately, because, as you keep horrific events in your mind, it only serves to attract and resonate with other horrific events in your experience, even if it is just a car accident, or a lost opportunity. If people were able to forget the past, when the past is negative, their present and future, would be so much brighter. 911, however, does serve as a powerful case study in Resonance, because there are so many related stories and events that we can now look back on and study.

Starting from the beginning, we know that everything from solid matter, to situations and events, are created from energy by their signature Frequencies. Frequencies, as you recall, have the power to shape energy into certain resulting forms, physical and non physical. Let's refer to the Video Example, Frequency Creates Shape, in the Chapter on Frequencies.

In that example, there was a pile of rice in the middle of the square metal sheet that was in no particular form or shape. However, as the frequency began to vibrate the rice, it started forming a certain pattern for that frequency. While each different frequency had a different pattern, if you repeated the experiment with the same frequency again, the same exact pattern would form and emerge again.

There are two important points to understand in regard to this example. First, the same frequency will always create the same exact pattern, and second, the pattern isn't clear at first. It takes time for the shape to form. If the power of the frequency were greater, (Higher Volume), it would form much faster. If the power of the frequency, Volume, were lower, it would take longer to take shape. So while a certain frequency will form the same pattern every single time, the speed at which it takes shape can very due to the power of the Frequency (Volume) and other circumstances.

Next, in review, we Know that while circumstances can be the same, their meanings can be different. In example, a building can be blown up and toppled to the ground, and that could be a good thing, if you are building a new Casino in that same location. However, a Building could be blown up resulting in a loss of property and possible a loss of life and that would be a bad thing. It's all in the Meaning and not the circumstance or event. It is the Meaning, that has a Resonant quality. It is the Meaning of a situation or event that is broadcast and transmitted to the Universe.

However, Meaning isn't always quite as clear cut as those two examples. While the meaning of the blowing up of the second building resulted in a loss of property, (Meaning = Bad), to the contractor who would eventually get the job to build a new building it would be a good Meaning. So in any given event or situation, there may be a thousand different Meanings going on that are resonating in a thousand different ways to each of the "Observers" who are each creating and establishing their own Meanings for the exact same event.

Now, let's revisit the Video Examples of the Dog, That Knew His Owner Was Coming Home. Remember in the dog example, the dog resonated with the Meaning of "HIS owner was now on the way home." If you were able to ask him how he knew this, he might say, "It was a gut feeling and I felt joy in my heart." Also, in that same Video, Rupert Sheldrake said that Cats know when their Owner intends to take them to the Veterinarian. No matter if the Owner calls the Vet from his work, or in his car, by the time he gets home, the cat is nowhere to be found. So while, the dog rejoices at the Meaning that he had received, the Cat, panics at the Meaning he received. If you were to ask the Cat how he knew that there was going to be a problem, he might say, "I just had a gut feeling that made me sick to my stomach."

So, if we look at these two examples of the Dog and the Cat, to see what they have in common, we will notice that while their Emotions were completely different, they were both heightened emotional responses, really great and really bad.

Chapter 5

In this next Video Example, you will learn about an Organization that is called the "Global Consciousness Project," [23] also known as the "EEG Project." They have deployed tiny little circuit boards all over the World to volunteers who are participating in this Global Experiment. These little devices are called "REGs," which stands for Random Event Generators. These little devices randomly generate a number "One" or a number "Zero," in the same way that you would flip a coin and get "Heads" or get "Tails." Just as you would expect, these little circuits normally average 50/50 ones and zeros, just like the odds that you would get flipping a coin.

Even though you would expect these hard wired computer circuits to always be consistent and generate the same results over and over again, it has been shown that they are affected by the Worlds "Emotional Energy." When Princess Diana died, at her funeral, there was such a Worldwide emotional feeling, that the REGs, "spiked" in one direction rather than the usual 50/50 split. There have been several other occasions, such as disasters, which caused the same results. It was the Heightened Emotional level that affected the REGs, not whether the Emotions were good or bad. Remember, it's not the level of emotion from one meaning, but all meanings together.

(23a) The Global Consciousness Project, also called the EGG Project, is an international, multidisciplinary collaboration of scientists, engineers, artists and others. The Global Consciousness Project, also called the EGG Project, is an international, multidisciplinary collaboration of scientists, engineers, artists and others. We collect data continuously from a global network of physical random number generators located in 65 host sites around the world. The archive contains 10 years of random data in parallel sequences of synchronized 200-bit trials every second. Our purpose is to examine subtle correlations that may reflect the presence and activity of consciousness in the world. **L274**

(23b) **Roger D. Nelson** is the director of the Global Consciousness Project (GCP), an international, multi-laboratory collaboration founded in 1997 to study collective consciousness. From 1980 to 2002, he was Coordinator of Research at the Princeton Engineering Anomalies Research (PEAR) laboratory at Princeton University. His professional focus is the study of consciousness and intention and the role of mind in the physical world. His work integrates science and spirituality, including research that is directly focused on numinous communal experiences. **L275**

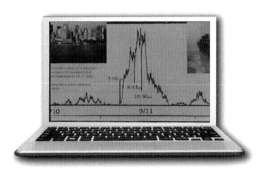

V276

Video Example World Consciousness Demonstrated

What is this video about?

This Video Example is a short news clip about the Global Consciousness Project (GCP). It is run by retired Princeton University Scientist, Dr. Rodger Nelson. He has deployed "Coin Flipping," Random Event Generators (REG) all over the World, to monitor the consciousness of the World's population. Although these electrical circuits are normally consistent in that they are generating flips that average 50% ones and 50% zeros, on occasion, they end up generating more of one than the other.

In the 10 years that this project has been in operation, there have been many World events that have caused a shift in these REGs from Random to mostly ones or zeros. The explanation for this is that a rise in the emotional energy of the World influences these electrical circuits to "polarize" or line up and become less random.

In the Video at two minutes and ten seconds (2:10), Dr. Nelson comments that several hours before the first plane hit the World Trade Center, there was a significant spike or shift in the randomness of these devices. He further states that he doesn't know why this occurred BEFORE the event had even become known to the World.

Clearly, the reason that there was a shift in the randomness BEFORE the first plane actually hit the tower is because the Meaning and the Frequency of the coming event was forming the circumstances of the event. Just like the Frequency and Rice example, even though the rice wasn't fully formed into the final pattern, you could hear the particular frequency, and if you are aware, you would know in your heart what pattern it is forming and you could respond at a subconscious or gut level.

Chapter 5

Like the sound of fingernails on a chalk board, certain Frequencies, can make you queasy and even sick to your stomach without even knowing why, and like the Cats, you respond and react automatically. Those REGs, were noticing the automatic resonance response from a World population that was aware at some level of consciousness that something bad was coming.

What does this example show and what does it mean?

This Video Example is very important, because it is not often that you have a way to measure and see the Resonant evidence at the very beginning of a situation or event while it's forming. Usually, all we notice is how everybody is upset, or happy, after the event has taken place. We don't notice or see them getting grumpier or happier as they are resonating with their own coming events. This Video Example shows us scientific evidence that something was happening and even though they don't know why it started before the first plane hit the tower, you do.

While the REGs were able to "Notice" something beginning a few hours before it actually happened, the actual Frequency started at the very moment that someone had the idea to do it. That could have been months or even years before.

 Like the Video Example of the Bridge that was twisting as it resonated with the sound of the wind through its suspension cables, the resonance of the coming event, wasn't noticed by the REGs until the situation had almost matured. However, if someone had their ear to the metal supports on the bridge, they could have heard it vibrating long before it could be seen vibrating.

Even though the REGs didn't register the coming event until it had almost matured and occurred, some people were able to notice this coming 911 event many days before it actually happened. In the next Video Example, you will meet Dave Edwards, a very "Lucky" man. He had just won the Jackpot on a Forty Two Million Dollar Power Ball Lottery. ($42,000,000).

Video Example Lottery Winner Survives 911   V278

What is this video about?

In this Video Example, Dave tells the story of how he won the Lottery [24] and had his life spared in the 911, attack. Because he was the big winner and a celebrity in his own right, he was invited to "Close the New York Stock Exchange." It is a big Honor, to be the one who slams the gavel down to end the trading day. Dave was scheduled to "Close the Exchange" on September 11, 2001.

The weekend before he was to fly into New York, he started getting sick to his stomach and had a feeling of great fear come over him. He called his stock broker to tell him that he wasn't going to be able to make it this time and would he please reschedule him for another time. The Stock broker got quite upset and was complaining because it had been so much trouble getting this set up in for him in the first place. Dave replied, "I know how crazy this is. I'm not coming to New York to close the Stock Exchange because I've got a weird feeling something bad is going to happen to me. Well I got the FEELING. I've never had it before, and I'm in the bathroom right now throwing my guts up. Now I'm not coming."

So on the morning of September 11, he got a frantic call from his stock broker shouting, "Turn on your TV!!!!!" So he turned it on in time to see the news from the first plane hitting the tower.

The Stock Broker continued, "I got a call from the guy at the New York Stock Exchange who was complaining that we weren't there. I told him that there was a memo that you were not going to be there.

Chapter 5

The man started shouting and said that you were supposed to be here right now…. Then the phone line went dead." The stock broker continued and said, "I just wanted to thank you, because I'm a father, and my boss is a father and we would have all died, had we gone."

What does this example show and what does it mean?

This Video demonstrates that like cats and dogs, people are able to sense resonance from coming events. Of course, like everything else, it all depends on how personally relevant the event is and how strong it is. Life and death events tend to be very strong, while a coming traffic ticket or a hang nail will be very small.

There are so many aspects of these series of events and these examples, that we can learn from and get a real strong understanding, belief and KNOWING.

In order to understand how people are able to pick up on psychic clues such as Resonance, we need to look at musically inclined people. In the example of the Frequency making Patterns in the Rice, we saw that different frequencies created different patterns. A musically inclined person would be able to recognize the different frequencies and call them a "B-Flat" for example. I am just picking names out of the air, because I'm not musically inclined. Let's say another Frequency is "A-Minor."

So when the "B-Flat" frequency is turned on, it creates a pattern we'll call "Aunt Sofia's Lace," and the "A-Minor," makes a pattern we call a "Snow Flake." In this way, he would have been able to establish a relationship between the sound of the frequency and the resulting pattern. This may be how the dog knows his owner is coming home, because whenever he gets a certain feeling, let's call it a "B-Flat," his owner shows up shortly thereafter. Pretty soon, whenever he gets that "Feeling," he gets excited because of the associated meaning. However, with the cat, that "Feeling" of an "A-Minor," means trouble and he runs and hides.

Like these dogs and cats, some people are able to notice Resonance and even interpret the "Feelings" quite accurately with the help of their Emotional Guidance System.

---

(24) PowerBall Lottery Information **L277**

The Future is Being Created, NOW!   C279

In the Video Example of the Dog Who Knew That His Owner Was Coming Home, from the dog's point of view, you might say that he was predicting the future, quite accurately in fact.

V256

Yet, from the Owner's point of View, it was just a decision he made in the present. Since our future is a cascading result of what is happening right now, it is easy to understand how some people can "See the Future," like the dog. If our musically inclined person, heard a certain frequency, noticed that there was a pile of rice on this vibrating metal surface, he could predict the exact pattern that would appear "In the Future," quite accurately.

There was a study done by parapsychologist William Cox, on train accidents in the U.S. He found that on the days that the trains had serious accidents, there were much fewer people on the train than would have normally been on the train on that same day in previous weeks. [25] This means that these people who for some reason decided not to take the train were actually responding to a gut feeling brought on by the Resonance of an upcoming accident. Remember, there is no such thing as an accident or a coincidence.

(25a) William E. Cox, "Precognition: An Analysis I and II," Journal of v American Society for Psychical Research 50 (1956).
(25b) Several More Interesting Stories - Bill Alcorn, Guest Speaker August 19, 2012 **L280**

Chapter 5

For those who felt good about their life and had a good outlook on life in general, their Reality would have prevented them from getting on that train. Maybe their car broke down on the way to the train station and they didn't make it, or maybe they got up late and missed the Train. Of course it could have been a straight forward gut feeling that they shouldn't take the train that day. It doesn't matter how the circumstance plays out, just that it does play out in a way that matches your Meanings. If you expect to be safe at all times, then "Things" will happen that end up keeping you safe. These "Things" and events are elicited from the sea of all possibilities by you, to create and fulfill the Meanings that you are transmitting.

Nothing can happen or does happen by "Accident" or "Coincidence." Prove it to yourself. Set up a Tuning Fork of any frequency that you want to and wait for it to vibrate. The moment that it begins to Vibrate, it will not only, not be an "Accident" because it will be vibrating in response to another vibration in the air that is similar, but, it won't be a "Coincidence" either because like frequencies always resonate with one another. That's what they do. That is the basis of the Creation of the Universe.

Now, let's get back to our Lottery Winner. He had just won $42 Million dollars and was feeling like everything was going great for him, like nothing could go wrong. From this wonderful feeling place, he was resonating with a lot of really great events that were coming his way. However, because he was already vibrating at such a high level of happiness, he didn't notice the other great things that were coming, because the Resonant feeling that they gave him, just blended in with the rest of the great things. However, when this really bad event began to resonate with him, he really noticed it because it was so different from the way he was feeling normally.

To use our guitar example, from earlier, he was vibrating on all those high strings, making beautiful music, when all of a sudden; there was this very loud sound of the low string that began to vibrate. It was so easy to notice because of the contrast it created. When he thought about his trip to N.Y., the sound got louder and its meaning resonated even stronger with his planned trip. He therefore correctly figured out that the cause of this uncomfortable Feeling (Vibration) was due to his trip, and so he canceled it. I'm sure that as soon as he canceled his trip, he began to feel much better.

However, for the person at the World Trade Center, that was expecting him to show up, it was business as usual. Even though, I don't have any specific information about him, I can tell you what his life was like. First he was yelling because the guy didn't show up. This was probably the kind of thing that happened to him all the time. He was a frustrated and unhappy person because of how he acted. His life wasn't what he wanted and he must have complained a lot. He had a lot of negative Meaning vibrations that he was sending out and as a result, he would have also "Received" (Noticed) the resonance of negative frequencies all the time. So when the frequency of this coming event started to resonate with him, it probably felt just like a normal day, of things not working out. That may have been why he was so mad. He could have mistaken the bad feeling that he was getting. He may have thought that it was because the Lottery Winner didn't show up like he was supposed to. If you are vibrating on the lower bad Frequencies most of the time (Playing low notes), how could you or would you notice that another low note is playing? It all seems similar to what you are used to and not unusual.

Chapter 5

All I know is this. Everybody who died, had that possibility in their energy. People, who notice the death and mayhem that plays throughout the World, accept that it is a part of life. "People get killed every day and my time could come at any moment." That kind of thinking, "Opens the door" to the death opportunities. Everybody who lived had survival in their energy. "Things are always working out for me." These kinds of people don't have the possibility of untimely death in their energy. They don't believe that we are all at risk and could be killed by a drunk driver, disease, or whatever, at any time.

There may have even been someone who totaled their car on the way to work that very morning, and while they were standing in the street looking at what once was a brand new car, uttered these words, "Even though, my car is totaled, I know that everything is still always working out for me in some way." Of course, they didn't make it to work at the World Trade Center that day, and they didn't die either.

This is where people exclaim that, "Good people died in that attack." I reply, "I know, they were wonderful and loving people, but, they also believed that there were things and people out there, who weren't loving and wonderful. They believed that they could be harmed and killed, whether it was by an accident, natural disaster, disease, or at the hands of another. They believed that there was a possibility that one day, it would be them." You could be "Mother Teresa," and still, if you thought about red cars, you would see them.

That's the kind of vibration you develop by watching the news every night and seeing and hearing that people died in a fire in their house, or in a car crash, or got shot at school or in a botched bank robbery, or by some mysterious disease. You begin to believe in the possibility of death whether you are a saint, or a scoundrel. When you know and understand, the matchmaking power of Resonance, you realize that when you are aware of death, death is aware of you. When you are aware of life, life is aware of you. When you are aware of happiness and opportunities, they are aware of you.

Chapter 5

192

In that train wreck example, not only were there people who didn't get on the Train on those "Accident" days, but there were people who did only on that day. I don't have any facts to show you, but it makes perfect sense. People who expect disaster, and misfortune, would have been attracted to take the Train on those days. Maybe they never take the Train, but just decided "For some Reason" to take the Train for once. Of course it crashed and they probably told their friends, "Can you believe it, I take the Train for the first time and sure enough, it wrecks on that day?" I can believe it. If they are experiencing events like that, and they keep talking about it, they are going to keep on eliciting and attracting more and more of them into their experience. Hopefully they will NEVER say, "One of these days one of these accidents is going to kill me," because if they do, it probably will.

If you hear on the news that someone has been breaking into houses, you begin to worry about it. You think, "Could it happen to me?" As you give thought to this, you are transmitting the meaning of "I could be robbed." When a thief drives through a neighborhood looking for his next victim, how do you think he decides which one he will rob? It is the one that he notices and which gives him a "Gut Feeling." Your house, which was once invisible to him, now catches the attention of this thief looking for a house to rob. He feels the resonance of your thought of being robbed and his desire to rob.

This explanation wasn't meant to scare you, and it doesn't happen that fast. However, what you think about often creates a "Normal" vibration for you and it will be responded to by the Universe through Resonance. When you become more careful about what you are paying attention to, and stop noticing things that don't serve you, your life begins to lighten up. For all you know, no one dies in your town, or the World. At least you haven't heard of it anyway, so it doesn't come to mind.

I had a friend of mine who told me that he had all this new security equipment and computer this and that. He said that it was very expensive and state of the art. I told him that he could never out run himself. The more security equipment he got, and the more sophisticated it became, the more he would need it, because he would be attracting and be coming to the attention of those who could defeat what he had.

Anything you guard against, you attract by Resonance. If you look at Warren Buffet, for example, who is worth about $50 Billion Dollars, you will find him walking through the store shopping just like any other person. He lives in a regular home in a regular neighborhood. He has no body guards nor does he worry about any potential problems, and as a result, he experiences a very safe life.

On the other hand, you will find executives who are worth much less money, with body guards and all the security that you can buy, and still they are threatened and experience close calls on their property and their person.

The problem is that if you don't have it, you will feel venerable, and from that place, you will attract problems. On the other hand, if you do employ security systems, you are still attracting problems. So, what is the answer?

You must align your actions and thoughts with your beliefs and still end up with a Meaning that will resonate only with what you want. If you feel you need the security, then get it, but use your GOD Power to change the Meaning of it. Say in your mind or to others, "I just have this security system because it gives me a discount on my insurance and makes it so that I don't have to worry about anything." From that place, you are sending out the Meaning that you have no concerns, there is no fear. However, if you put in the security system and say to yourself or even to others, "I got this security system, because I'm afraid and I'm protecting myself from all the bad people who might try to harm me." Then you are sending out a Meaning that you expect that someone is going to harm you and that you could experience harm at the hands of another. From that place you light up like a beacon to those who are looking for someone like you.

In the wild, do you know how a predator spots its prey? The prey looks and acts like prey. That's what attracts their attention and notice.

C281

You Don't Need to Figure Out What Went Wrong

It is not important to figure out or discover what went wrong in any situation because, nothing has gone wrong. How can something go wrong, if you control the Meaning? If something has gone wrong, that means that you haven't used your GOD Power "Yet" to change the Meaning to something going right. The actual situation or event is of no consequence and doesn't matter. It is only the Meaning that counts.

Meaning trumps situation every single time. Besides, if you go about thinking and considering what might have gone wrong, you are only bringing it to mind again and you are going to elicit it all over again because of your thoughts. There is nothing worse than hearing someone brainstorming on what when wrong. They start naming all kinds of things, and end up building a strong case as to why it should go wrong and why it will go wrong again. Why would you think of all these bad causes just to give them energy? The really bad thing about this kind of approach is, that you end up thinking of so many more new reasons that weren't even the cause, but now that they have been brought up and are on your mind, they could be the cause of the next problem.

When something has occurred, you are in a new and different place than where you were before. Nothing is the same. What may or may not have gone wrong, doesn't matter, because you have a new and different view point now, that you are going to build on. Don't think of the reasons that something might have gone wrong, think of the opportunities that you have now that you are "here."

Chapter 5

If you assert a meaning that everything has worked out in a way that will end up being the best possible situation, then from here, you will begin to see new possibilities that you could have never seen, if you start all over again from the place of "it failed." If it has instead succeeded in some way, which you may not even be aware of just yet, then you are on a whole new path going in a new direction. Since everything is always working, if you say it is, then you will use Resonance to elicit the perfect new options from the Universe in response to your successful situation. Many a failure in the past has lead to amazing and profitable discoveries and opportunities. Many an adversity has suddenly turned around and become the greatest possible situation they could have ever wanted, and it was as a result of a "Failure" that turned into a success. At this point, let me give you my definition of "Adversity."

P001

"Adversity Is A Sudden Change In Direction On A Need To Know Basis"

R.L.M.

Until this moment, you didn't need to know. If you had, you might have changed something or done something differently, and then you wouldn't have arrived at this most opportune moment in your life. You will find that many of the greatest achievements known to man came through a moment of adversity, and if anything had changed prior to that, and that moment of adversity had not occurred, those achievements would have never been born. Often the greatest adversities become the greatest blessings. Do not search for what went wrong or what is wrong; instead search for what went right and what is right now.

GOD Does Not, and Cannot, Judge You   C282

I just wanted to cover this topic as thoroughly as possible before we end this chapter on Resonance. Many people believe that GOD, the Universe, or some Higher Power, somehow judges them in one way or the other. That is not the case at all. While I have covered this concept and understanding several different times thus far, and I will be touching on it some more throughout the rest of this book, I just want to explain it directly, right now as we are discussing Resonance.

The Universe or GOD if you will, has no function, mechanism, or system that can Punish or Reward anyone. The only function or system that operates in the Universe is Resonance, which elicits its "Kind" or "Match" into existence. What you get or don't get, experience or don't experience is a function of Resonance. How can you experience anything in your Life that you did not elicit through Resonance? It is impossible. You can only see and experience what you are in Resonance with, in some way.

If you FEEL GOOD about something that you did or are thinking, you will see and elicit things that you like and want into your experience. You could think of this as being "Rewarded" by GOD, but, it is in fact only Resonance eliciting GOOD Things into your experience because they "Match" your Good Thoughts and Deeds. On the other hand, if you FEEL BAD about something that you did or are thinking, you will see and elicit things that you don't like and don't want into your experience. You could think of this as being "Punished" by GOD, but, it is in fact only Resonance eliciting BAD Things into your experience because they "Match" your Bad Thoughts and Deeds. It is always YOU that is the "Cause" and/or the "Creator" of your own experience. It is you that decides if you have been Good or Bad as you define it. As a result of YOUR OWN JUDGMENT, you will reap the Consequences or the Rewards of your thoughts and actions.

Remember the Video-Example "A Past Life Regression Expert," back in Chapter #2, The Meaning of Your Life, where Michael Newton describes his work in Past Life Regression. In that Video, he says that when people are planning their next Life Experience, they will often choose to be the victim of a crime in their next experience if they were the perpetrator of a crime in their last Life. How can they be the "Victim" if there is no one willing to be the perpetrator? They are trying out different experiences in their Physical Lives. He also stresses that there is NO JUDGMENT whatsoever during the time in between lives.

Later on in the book in Chapter 10. The Reality of Your Body as a Representation, Video Example – "The Day I Died" Vicki Noratuk's Story, & Video Example – Near Death Experience Explained, you will hear personal stories of people who had Near Death Experiences, where they had a chance to find out what it was like in the non-physical realm. EVERY SINGLE ONE OF THEM, stated that is was a place of pure LOVE and total acceptance. There was no criticism or judgment what so ever. How can there be? You are a sovereign, immortal, non-physical Being who is experimenting and experiencing what it is like to "Play" different parts in a physical Human form.

Like a video game, if you "Die" or get killed in this incarnation, you are out of the game and this experience. And, like a video game you have unlimited lives and can play the game over and over again in any way you wish. While you are in the non-physical realm, you are planning your next entry into the game and experience of Human Life. You are busy planning your next life including what Body you will use and what major experiences you will line up for yourself. If those experiences weren't wrong while you were still in non-physical form, planning them for the future, then how could they be "Wrong" when they play out while you are in physical form? They can't. You can think that they are, and who knows, that may be part of your "Planned Experience." BUT, in the REAL REALITY of the Universe, nothing is wrong; it is all just an experience. Remember we are all Non-Physical Immortal Beings, playing physical beings for the fun and experience of it. Nothing has lasting consequences because nothing is Real. It is all just energy being shaped by Meaning for the Fun and Experience of it all.

Now, I have to say that if it is important to you to "Believe" that there is some Higher Judgment, that is your "Decision." It is not my place to condemn or commend your decisions as they pertain to your own Reality. That is your Business. I would only like to point out that as you give that responsibility away to GOD or the Universe to judge you, praise you, and condemn you, you lessen your own power to Create and Control your own experience. If on the other hand, you recognize that it is your own Judgment of yourself that is affecting and influencing your life, then you can take total control of your own life.

In summary, if you feel bad about something, don't worry that there is some "Higher Judgment," there is not. However, YOUR OWN JUDGMENT does have REAL consequences. If you think that something is Bad or Wrong, then it is for you. If you think that something is not, then it isn't, for you. If you feel bad about yourself for something that you have done or thought, then You need to release your Guilt and self condemnation so that you will not be eliciting more problems into your experience through Resonance. There are several sections in this Book that will show you how to release your Guilt and feel better about yourself.

Chapter 5

C283   Now, Prove It!

As I have said again and again, this book is all about KNOWING! Just Believing and Accepting is not enough. I want you to KNOW this information is TRUE and REAL! If you want to change your Reality and be able to effectively exercise your GOD Power, you have to be operating at a higher Consciousness Level where you KNOW how the Universe works and where you can create any Experience that you want for yourself. Now that I have said all that, when I tell you that Resonance will Elicit information and create events in your Experience, I don't want you to just take my word for it. I want you to find out for yourself by PROVING IT! There is a simple exercise that you can do that will easily Prove that Resonance is working for you and that it is just as amazing as it sounds in its ability to find what you want and bring it to your attention. This exercise involves the "Noticing" of Numbers that are 3 of a kind. This would be everything from 000, 111, 222, 333, and up to 999. After you have "Practiced Noticing" these numbers they will suddenly appear all the time in your experience.

Step #1. Start looking for every opportunity to see three numbers in a row. That would be like your clock is at say 2:15, so you keep watching it until it gets to 2:22. You notice the time clock on the Football game is at

4:55 seconds to go, so you watch it count down until it reaches 4:44. You notice that your speedometer is just about to reach a triple number so you keep looking back at it until you "Catch" it on a triple number. You are at the store looking at prices and you begin to notice $9.99. Keep noticing these numbers. Go out of your way to notice them, no matter what it takes. Make it a sport to find them and spot them.

Step #2. Start noticing that you are noticing these triple numbers. Sure you are looking for them on purpose, but, start noticing that you just happen to look up at the clock for no special reason and notice 5:55, or 11:11. As you start noticing that you are noticing triple numbers "Unexpectedly" you begin to realize that there is no "Logical" reason that you would have seen them. You recognize that you haven't looked at the clock all day, but the moment that you do, it is 3:33, or the countdown timer on the Microwave is at 4:44. You could never have seen that number by "Planning" it. You think to yourself "I just happened to look up and there it was! What a coincidence!" But it wasn't a "Coincidence." It was your "Meaning Frequency" of "Seeing Triple Numbers," that was Resonating with the "Situation" and brought it to your attention because it was "Relevant" to your desires. You "Wanted to see triple Numbers and Resonance brought them to your attention. From now on, as long as you have the "Active" Vibration (Meaning), that you want to see triple numbers, Resonance will bring them to your attention. Every time they are in the area, you will just "Happen" to notice them everywhere!

Now that you KNOW Resonance is a REAL force that can work for you, what do you want to notice? Opportunity? The Perfect Mate? A new Home, new job, or whatever else. Start practicing looking for what you want and noticing it as often as you can, and soon the Vibration will not only be "Active," but it will be powerfully Resonating with these things you want in your Experience and making you turn your head, or pick up the phone, or look in the paper, or turn on the TV just in time to see and find just want you are looking for and just the right time.

Chapter 5

C284   Chapter 5 Resonance, The Secret

"Match-Making" Force Of The Universe

- Chapter Review –

* Resonance is two "Similar Frequencies" interacting and mutually stimulating each other. Similarity of the Frequencies is determined by the "Meanings" that created them.

* Resonance elicits a response that is Automatic, Irresistible, and Absolute.

* Resonance can exert and elicit a force equal to the "Magnitude of the Situation" or the "Total Mass of the Object."

* Resonance is a "Primary Force" that is above and beyond any and all "Manifested Forces" such as Gravity, Time, Heat, Electricity, Nuclear, Magnetism etc.

* Resonance is a "Pervasive Force" in that is not limited by time or distance.

* Resonance is the Second Most Powerful Force in the Universe, After Meaning & Frequency, because it is a "Responding" Force. Meaning is a "Primary" force because it initiates actions and events.

* Resonance is the "Action" of Creation. Once the Frequency has been created, Resonance goes to work Matching & Eliciting the appropriate Responses.

Chapter 5 Resonance, The Secret   C285

"Match-Making" Force Of The Universe

- Chapter Quiz -

1) Resonance is a state when what occurs?

A) Like Frequencies Meet

B) Un-Like Frequencies Meet

C) Frequency Meets Energy

D) A Situation meets Matter

2) Resonance has the ability to do what?

A) Move huge masses   B) Elicit Responses From Like Frequencies

C) Bring into a mutual awareness people, situations and events

D) All

3) Resonance is a "Primary Force" second only to:

A) Electrical Force

B) Nuclear Force

C) Meanings & Their Frequencies

D) Gravity

4) Resonance has the power to:

A) Elicit a Specific Result from a Situation B) Create Mutual Awareness

C) Elicit Responses From Any Distance or Time   D) All

5) Resonance can be best described as:

A) The Universal Matchmaker B) Always Working & Always Effective

C) The "Enforcer" That Carries Out Your Meanings   D) All

See All The Quiz Answers (Page 227)

A285

A286

A287

Chapter 5

C852   Read This Book Again

You think that you got a lot from it the first time through, just wait and see what you will get in the next read! Remember that you only elicit and experience that which is within your own Reality. I know that most of this information was outside your Reality on the first read through. As a result, you might have read it, but, you have not really processed it into your Reality yet, not completely. However, some of it did "get in" and has in fact altered your point of view. When you read this book again, you will now be reading it and processing it from a new point of view, with new beliefs, that are much higher up from where you were the first time through. From this new perspective you will get an even higher and deeper understanding than you could have gotten the first time through, even if you studied it thoroughly.

Each time you read it, you will be eliciting evidence into your experience that confirms its validity. From that new place of higher belief, you will gain even more KNOWING and understanding. No matter how many times you read this book, you will get new and better understandings and your confidence in your own GOD Power will be stronger and stronger until you are the Absolute MASTER of your own Reality and your own life!

"As You *BECOME* A More Advanced Student,

This Will *BECOME* an even More Advanced Course"

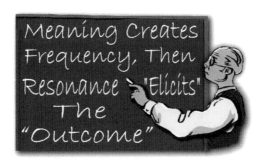

Teach This Material to Someone   C853

There is only one other way to gain an even better and deeper Understanding of this amazing material, and that is to teach it and share it with others in your Life. I don't mean to pass on this book to others to read, although that would be good too, but to actually verbally explain what you have read and what you KNOW to others. It could be your Family and Friends, Work Associates, Study Groups, or even civic or other speaking opportunities. As you form the ideas in your mind to speak them, they come from a different place, one that is a place of KNOWING, from the passive, to the active places in your mind and thinking. You don't have to be a great "Teacher" to share this KNOWLEDGE, just explain it the best that you can. It will invariably lead to a discussion that will heighten your understanding and KNOWING. If you want, you can just read part of it, a few pages and then explain them, read a few more and explain them. It is in your explaining that you deepen your understanding and greater KNOWING occurs.

If you don't have anyone to explain it to, then explain it to yourself in writing or on tape or just speak it out loud in a quiet place where you have some privacy. How about having your inner discussion with yourself, in the park on a beautiful day, or at the Beach, or in your favorite reading chair with your favorite music playing softly in the background.

Maybe you aren't ready to get to the teaching part yet. Fine, then just read it again and maybe after you finish the book for the second time, you will have the confidence and KNOWING to share what you have learned with others. If not, Read it again. At some point, you will feel so good about what you know and the improvements in your own life that you will want to shout it from the roof tops! I'll be listening for those glorious shouts of utter JOY... Thank You!

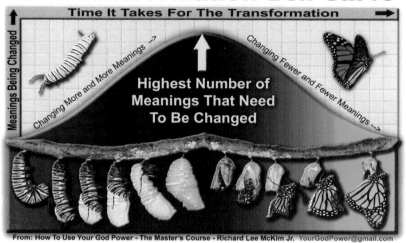

From: How To Use Your God Power - The Master's Course - Richard Lee McKim Jr. YourGodPower@gmail.com

Implementation And Transformation

This is a breakdown of what to expect when implementing the God Power Philosophy. Of course the core of the God Power Philosophy is changing the Meanings of situations to improve their Reality. First, let's get a clear understanding of what it Means to experience a Transformation which can be explained by the life cycle of a Butterfly.

The Butterfly first starts out as a Caterpillar. In this early stage of life, the Caterpillar has a limited perspective as it crawls from place to place eating leaves. Of course it has no idea what it is missing or what kind of Life it will soon have.

Once the Caterpillar Transforms into a Butterfly, life is quite different. The Butterfly is able to fly high above any and all problems, and see the World from as much higher and broader perspective. You might call this a Higher Consciousness point of view, seeing  the Trees as well as the Forest. The Butterfly spends its days fluttering between Beautiful Flowers and feasting on tasty nectar.

Your Transformation follows a similar path. In the beginning, life is difficult and obstacles seem insurmountable. While it seems like you Know everything that you need to know, your perspective and level of consciousness is quite limited in the big picture.

However, after you have experienced your personal Transformation into a new and better life, You wonder why you waited so long to get to this place utter joy and pure bliss. As you look around your World, you see the perfection in everything. Your Higher Consciousness allows you to soar high above problems and obstacles and see the "Bigger Picture." Food tastes Better, people are nicer, money and love come easily. Life BECOMES "Effortless" and fun.

The Hallmark of Transformation is that:

"It is An Irreversible & Permanent Change"

These changes which lead to your Transformation follow the standard Bell Curve that we have all heard about. Looking at the Illustration, Going from left to right, is the Length of Time from the time you first read this Book until the time when your Transformation is complete.

At first, you will begin to notice small situations and events changing almost automatically just because of your new understanding. This is the very Beginning stages of your Transformation. You will change a few Meanings and notice that "It is Working!" Of course this leads to more and more Meaning Changes, with more and more improvement in your Reality.

Eventually, you will reach the top of the curve where you are aware of and consciously changing more Meanings than you will ever have to change again. During this time, you are experiencing so many great results and favorable events and circumstances manifesting into your life.

However, after you pass the peak of your Meaning changes, (The Middle of the Curve) you will be changing fewer and fewer Meanings. This is because you are experiencing fewer and fewer events and circumstances that need to have their Meanings changed. More and more things are working out already by themselves without the need for a change in Meaning. These are the final stages of your Transformation.

Soon, there will come a time when EVERYTHING is already, and automatically working out. At this stage of your Transformation, you are incapable of seeing anything as "Going Wrong." Your Transformation is Complete! Congratulations on a Job well done.

Do You Want To Help Change The World?

The only reason that there are problems in the World is because people are not getting what they want. If everyone were able to get what they wanted and live the Life of their Dreams, they would be happy and content. It would be a wonderful World for EVERYONE!

We know that there is plenty to go around because Abundance is not something that is taken from another, it is something that is CREATED and ELICITED from the Universe.

So how can YOU help change the World and improve it for yourself, your children, and generations to come? It is so simple. You cannot FORCE People to change and think differently, but, you can teach them how to get what they want.

As mentioned in the section *"Teach This Material To Others,"* there is a level of learning that can only be reached by teaching others. When you explain this information in your terms, you own it, and truly understand it at a deeper level and your KNOWING skyrockets. By helping others, you help yourself.

Teach this material to others. Show them how to get what they want in a way that does not harm themselves or others. When people think that things are going wrong for them, they are angry, depressed and lash out at others. Of course, when you think that things are not working out for you, you naturally Elicit more unhappiness and life becomes harder.

If only they knew, that expecting things to work out, elicits perfect solutions, and reveals hidden opportunities for success and happiness. Things could improve so easily for most people with just a little help in understanding how they are actually creating their own Reality.

Teach them that all they have to do is change the MEANING of the events and situations in their life, and then look for the things that are working out for them. Share the God Power Philosophy with them and send the God Power Philosophy Illustration to them.

Since the Movie *"The Secret"* came out, there are Millions of people who are looking for more information and the exact step by step way to implement the Law of Attraction. This is where you can play your part in Changing the World by teaching this valuable information to the others in your life. The God Power Philosophy is both about Self Help and Helping Others. I have given you all the tools that you need to do this.

#1) The entire course is on YouTube for FREE, where anyone in the World can learn how to improve their own lives. All you have to do is share the links in this Book on your websites, Blogs, Tweets, FaceBook postings and by Email to the ones you care about. I have even created an "On-Line Guide" to the Master's Course that has links to the Online Videos and Course Resources.

Get the Free On-Line Guide to the "Master's Course" Here:

www.TinyURL.com/DownloadCourseGuide **L860**

#2) I have created nearly one hundred course Illustrations that you can post on any website and send to anyone in the World. They are all FREE of charge to anyone who wants them. Download all the Course Illustrations Here:

www.PhotoBucket.com/YourGodPower **L861**

www.TinyURL.com/DownloadPictures **L862**

#3) I have created Review points and Questions at the end of each Chapter for Review and Discussion. These Questions make it easy to learn the material and share it with others in discussion groups. [129]

You can join a study group online on in your local community or even start one yourself. There are several Websites that are devoted to helping people of like minds get together to further their own causes. [130]

You could post comments on Blogs and Forums with your thoughts, personal experiences and to offer help to those who are seeking it.

This topic is very important to me. That is why I have provided my entire Master's Course On-Line for FREE. I will do what I can to support Your efforts to Help/Change the World.

Let me know about your Group/ Forum/ Blog/ Website where you are Discussing and Promoting the God Power Philosophy, and I will include it in a list for others to find.

"May You Wake One Day To Find
That Your Life Is Everything
You Ever Wanted It To Be"

Sincerely

Richard Lee McKim Jr.

_____

(129) A study group is a small group of people who regularly meet to discuss shared fields of study. These groups can be found in high school and college settings and within companies. Professional advancement organizations also may encourage study groups. Each group is unique and draws on the backgrounds and abilities of its members to determine the material that will be covered. Often, a leader who is not actively studying the material will direct group activities. **L863**

(130) Meetup is the world's largest network of local groups. Meetup makes it easy for anyone to organize a local group or find one of the thousands already meeting up face-to-face. More than 9,000 groups get together in local communities each day, each one with the goal of improving themselves or their communities. Meetup's mission is to revitalize local community and help people around the world self-organize. Meetup believes that people can change their personal world, or the whole world, by organizing themselves into groups that are powerful enough to make a difference. **L864**

Learn more on the **L865**

Create a Meet-Up Study Group **L866**

Join The God Power Community

These Materials and Understandings are More Advanced than what is generally available, so, it is important to be able to <u>Connect With Others</u> who are on the same path as you. For that reason, We have created the *God Power Community* for those on this path of Enlightenment.

There will be Special Gatherings, Private Webinars, Tele-Seminars, and Offerings only available to the Members of the *God Power Community*.

Anyone seeking Enlightenment and wanting to improve their lives are welcome to join us. Simply send an E-Mail to the address provided (Below) and ask to be included in the *God Power Community*.

YourGodPower@gmail.com

C870 Appendix A

A Tribute to Michael Talbot

Author of "The Holographic Universe"

Michael Talbot wrote the bestselling book "The Holographic Universe." I bought the book many years ago and just never got around to reading it. Perhaps it wasn't time for me to read it until now. As we know everything is "Elicited" into action and actuality at just the right time, not a moment before or after. Frankly, it was just after I finished "Digesting" his book that I began to outline this book.

"The Holographic Universe," was just one of his many books that he wrote, but it was his most noteworthy. In it he promotes the idea that the Universe is "Holographic" in nature and is just a 3-d Projection similar to the Holographic image projections you see in the movies and at the theme parks. He made it his mission to explain the benefits of this knowledge through his interviews and public appearances.

After I read his book, I was so excited about the examples and this insight into the workings of the Universe that I wanted to meet him in person and discuss these concepts in depth. However, much to my dismay, I found out that he had died many years before and this "Meeting of the Minds" was never to be.

He was a "Master" of unearthing interesting facts and sources that most people would never be able to find. In his Master Piece, he has cited 530 References!!! That is an amazing amount of research. Most people would never be able to find all those sources and information. However, he had an advantage over most people. He was a firm believer in the supernatural and had personal experiences all his life with such things as "poltergeist" and "Seeing" what others could never see. It was because of his belief and faith in the supernatural that he was able to elicit, find and discover these hard to find stories and information of amazing Realities from around the World.

While I have included a handful of his stories and references in this book, it pales in comparison to the vast wealth of stories and references available in his book. It is your great fortune, that you can read this book first to expand your Reality into include the amazing, and then to read Michael's Book, "The Holographic Universe," to expand your thinking even more. You may never have read his book before because you were not eliciting that kind of information into your experience, but now that you are, it will prove to be quite valuable to you in your quest for "KNOWING."

"Thank You Michael for your wonderful book and contribution to my KNOWING."

Sincerely,

Richard Lee McKim Jr.

C875 # Appendix B

I Need Your Input For My Next Book

I am finding that I am now "Eliciting" amazing stories from people all over the World. As I expand my own Reality to include more and more amazing things and experiences, I am "Eliciting" more and more of them into my experience. I love it!!

Until now, most of the stories and hard to believe facts that were disclosed in this book would never have come your way. However, now that your mind and Reality have been expanded, you will begin to discover more and more amazing abilities in yourself and others. I want to hear about your amazing stories and abilities and even those of others that you know or have heard about. Remember, it is the "Idea" of it that is the most valuable. I am thinking about writing another book on amazing "GOD Power" Stories to further expand my Reader's minds as to what is possible. I am interested in anything that you know personally or have heard about from others.

Michael Talbot said that as a child he was able to see two Moons in the sky until someone told him that it wasn't real. I had a friend of mine tell me that when she was a little girl she levitated and it scared her. Another friend of mine told me that he threw a marble "Through" a wall as a kid and had to go around into the other room to get it. These kinds of amazing things are happening all the time.

I want to hear about them so that I can share them with growing number of enlightened people around the World who KNOW how the Universe really works. I won't share any personal information, just the story itself. I am also interested in Hypnosis stories and even successful Hypnosis "Scripts" that I can share with my Readers to help them expand their Personal Realities even more. Anything that you think would be interesting, Please send it.

Anyone who sends me a story, information, or just requests it, I will include you on a special Contact list to receive updates on interesting information that may be useful to your Reality Expansion work.

Send them to:

YourGodPower@gmail.com

Thank You,

Sincerely,

Richard Lee McKim Jr.

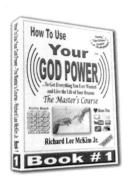

How To Use Your God Power
"The Master's Course"
6"x 9" Paperback - 228 Pages
20 Video Examples - 537 Links
(Audio Book Download Included - 12 CDs)

Chapter 1 - Your GOD Power - This Chapter Explains what Your God Power is and Gives Several Real Life Examples of God Power In Action to Create Both Beneficial and Detrimental Results.

Chapter 2 - The Meaning of Life (Your Life) - It Explains What Your Life Purpose Is and Why You Became A Physical Human Being Here on Planet Earth.

Chapter 3 - The Most Powerful Formula in Your Life - This Chapter Sets Forth a Perfect Life Formula That Will Always Work To Keep Your Life Experience Happy, Successful, and Satisfying.

Chapter 4 - Frequencies And Meaning - This Chapter Explains That Meanings Have Certain Frequencies. When These Frequencies Are Added Together, They Create Everything From an Atom, To Your Life Experience and Even The Entire Universe

Chapter 5 - Resonance, The Secret Match-Making Force Of The Universe - It Explains The Concept of "Resonance" which is the Basis of "The Law Of Attraction." Resonance is a Primary Force of The Universe, Second Only to Meaning.

Paperback Edition: L921   **Kindle Edition: L924**

How To Use Your God Power
"The Master's Course"
6"x 9" Paperback - 336 Pages
26 Video Examples - 852 Links
(Audio Book Download Included - 17 CDs)

Chapter 6 - The Power of Labels - This Chapter Explains How Powerful Labels Are And How To Use Them in a Beneficial way To Create Your Reality You Want.

Chapter 7 - You Must Decide - This Chapter Explains That Decision And The Subsequent Alignment With That Decision, Is One Of The Most Important Foundational Techniques Reality Creation. Make A Decision and Align with it.

Chapter 8 - What is Reality? - This Chapter Explains The Concept Of "Reality." What Is Reality? There is Not One Overall Reality. We Each Have Our Own Individual Realities That We Form and Shape Ourselves. No Reality can Interfere with another's Reality.

Chapter 9 - The Reality of Your Life Experience - This Chapter explains what part Religion Plays in Reality Creation and answers the Question whether our Lives are governed by our own Free Will or destined by Fate.

Chapter 10 - The Reality of Your Body as a Representation - Our Bodies do not function like Machines, that they are in fact just a representation, a projection, a result of our thoughts. A change in our thoughts can and does result in an actual physical change in our body, good or bad.

Paperback Edition: L931   Kindle Edition: L934

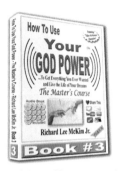

How To Use
Your God Power
"The Master's Course"
6"x 9" Paperback - 244 Pages
15 Video Examples - 552 Links
(Audio Book Download Included - 13 CDs)

Chapter 11 - The Reality of Your Emotions - This Chapter explains that our Emotions are a Powerful Guidance System. While our Emotions do not create in themselves, they do indicate the power and direction of our creations.

Chapter 12 - Changing Your Own Reality - This Chapter Explains the different ways that we can actually alter our Realities. It includes 10 Video examples that help to demonstrate the possibilities of Hypnosis, Psychedelic Drugs, as well as stories and examples of altered Realities.

Chapter 13 - The Reality of The Skeptic And The Doubter - This Chapter Explains that while the "Skeptic" is a Master of Reality Maintenance, his opinions and points of view are only valid within his own Reality and have no basis in Yours. You have the ability to think and do things that the Skeptic cannot even imagine, and therefore outside his Reality.

Chapter 14 - What Is Theoretically Possible in Your Own Reality - It sets forth amazing thoughts & ideas of what is possible. Learn directly from another's mind, living or dead. Change your body to match the one you had in a 10 year old photo. Create a "Magical" Home Pharmacy that automatically turns candy into powerful medicines.

Chapter 15 - Conclusion - This Chapter brings together all the powerful concepts taught in the course and clearly demonstrates that you can Use Your God Power to Get Everything You Ever Wanted and Live The Life Of Your Dreams.

Paperback Edition: L941   Kindle Edition: L944

How To Use Your God Power Products

How To Use Your God Power Master's Course DVD-ROM

- 555 Page Fully Integrated E-Book - Illustrations - Video Links
- 35+ Hour Audio Book – Fully Integrated with the E-Book
- 1,500 Slide Power Point Presentation Fully Integrated
- 51+ Hour Flash Movie Presentation - Fully Integrated
- Over 100 Video Examples Referred to by Internet Links
- Over 100 Illustrations and Animations - Fully Integrated
- Links to over 100 Video Examples (15 Hours) **L901**

How To Use Your God Power Master's Course - 40 CD Audio Book

- Entire Course Recorded on 40 Audio CDs
- Each CD Has an Information Track That Explains What it Covers •The Course Is Recorded on 36 CDs and Includes 4 Bonus Review CDs!

L903

How To Use Your God Power Master's Course - 18 DVD (9 Box) Set

- Entire Course in a 9-Box, 18 DVDs
- The Course is Nearly 40 Hours Long
- The 18 DVDs + Bonus Review DVD!
- Course Chapters are Divided into Easy To Watch Segments **L904**

How To Use Your God Power Master's Course With The 30 Day, Habit Breaking, High Intensity Training/Coaching One on One

Tired Of Not Getting Ahead? Confused By The Barrage Of Conflicting Advice? Do You Want To Be Able To Actually Collect Your Share From The Abundance of The Universe? Are You Ready To Take Action Right Now, and Be Creating The Life Of Your Dreams In 30 Days Or Less? If So, Then You Need This 30 Day High Intensity, God Power Training. L910

This High Intensity Training Is The ONLY Way To Quickly And Effectively Change Your Life. You Will Have 30 Consecutive Days of One On One Coaching and Intensive Training Directly with Richard Lee McKim Jr. Himself. This Special Training is Designed to Break ALL of Your Old Ineffective Habits and Create New Powerful Habits that Will Automatically Transform Your Life. You Will Learn How To Use Your God Given Power, To Change Your Reality, On A Daily Basis, To Get Everything You Ever Wanted and Live The Life Of Your Dreams. Every Single Day Will Be Reviewed & Discussed To Insure Success. Expect To See Positive Results Fast. Most Start Seeing Positive Results With In Just A Few Days Of Starting This High Intensity Training. This Intensive Coaching Will Continue With Follow up Calls and Regular Contact to Insure That You Are Successfully Using Your New Skills.

Home Study Materials: This is The Complete How To Use Your God Power Master's Course. It comes with 40 Hours of Video on 18 DVDs. It Includes The Complete Audio Book on 40 CDs. It also has the 1500 Slide Power Point Presentation of The Course and Another 40 Hours of Video in The SWF Interactive Format.

NOTICE: Do To The Intense Nature Of This Powerful Training, There Will Only Be A Few Openings. This Training Is Success Driven and Designed To Create A Life Long Change In 30 Days Or Less. If You Really Want A Positive Change In Your Life Quickly, And Are Willing To Go The Distance And Do The Work, This Is The Program For You.

L910

Your Likes, Comments, *And* Review of This Book Are Very Important And Greatly Appreciated!

Richard Lee McKim Jr.

We live in an amazing and wonderful time in history. Never has Your Opinion been more Wanted and Appreciated, nor has it ever mattered as much as it does now. After all, who else's opinion could matter more than someone who has read this Book?

Word of Mouth has always been a key factor for making decisions. Amazon knows how Important Your Opinion is to others and has made it super easy for you to share Your Valuable Comments with the World.

Post a Comment and Review by clicking on the *Write a customer review* "Button" on The Amazon Book Page: **L921** Or you could use This Customer Review Direct Link to write a Review right from this Book!

Post a Review/Comment for this Book: L925

Importantly, Your Likes, Comments, and Review of this book will live on as a Sign Post to those who discover this Book after You. Future Readers are depending on You to guide them to the Important and Valuable Books that they should Read. By leaving a Comment and Review, You will forever be connected to this Book and become an important part of its success.

Sincerely,

Richard Lee McKim Jr.

"Thank You For Your Valuable Comments & Book Review"

Chapter 1 Your GOD Power   C143

Chapter Quiz The Correct Answers Are Highlighted

1) When it says that we were made in the "Image" of GOD, what does that mean?

A) We look like him

B) We can think

C) We have a certain ability/power

D) None

2) What does Your GOD Power give you the ability to do?

A) Change Meanings

B) Change Your Situation

C) Get Well

D) All

3) What do we have that animals do not?

A) Senses

B) Physical Experiences

C) Ability to Think & Decide

D) Ability to Change Reality

4) What is the foundational basis of every single experience?

A) The Actual Physical Elements & Characteristics of the Experience

B) The Underlying Meaning of the Experience

5) Does the idea of GOD Power make since in terms of Religion, Physics, Psychology & Biology?

A) Yes

B) No

Quiz Answers And Chapter Review

C172   Chapter 2 The Meaning of Life (Your Life)

Chapter Quiz The Correct Answers Are Highlighted

1) Your arrival here on Earth, can best be described as:

A) An Accident   B) A Well Thought Out, Purposefully Planned Event

C) A Completely Random event   D) A freak occurrence

2) In the Point "A" to Point "B" example, Your Point "A" refers to what?

A) Your Birth   B) The starting place of a journey of experience

C) A new decision   D) All of These

3) Your Physical Life Experience can be best described as:

A) An accidental result of evolution   B) Haphazard life combination

C) Playing a chosen character, that is actually experiencing their "part" as a real-life Experience

4) In the Camp Activity Example, it states that you are here for what?

A) To experience the activities of your choice

B) To get something done that needs to be done

5) The concept of "Immersion" can best be described as:

A) The complete and utter focus on your physical experience to the exclusion of all else

B) Remembering your nonphysical abilities and your history from before your birth

Quiz Answers And Chapter Review

A172

A173

Chapter 3 The Most Powerful Formula In Your Life

(The "Platinum" Formula)   C186

Chapter Quiz The Correct Answers Are Highlighted

"Everything Is Working Out For You If You Know It Is."

1) In this formula, what does "Everything" refer to?

A) Your Finances

B) Your Personal Life

C) Your Health

D) All of Them

2) In this formula, what does "Working Out" mean?

A) Getting Better

B) Staying The Same

C) Getting Worse

D) None

3) In this formula, who is "Everything Working Out" For?

A) Your Neighbor

B) Your Best Friend

C) Your Mother

D) You

4) In order for this formula to work, who has to be the one who "KNOWS" that everything is working out?

A) Your Neighbor

B) Your Best Friend

C) Your Mother

D) You

5) What does it mean to KNOW something?

A) You're Doubtful

B) You Wonder About it

C) You Hope it is

D) You are Certain

Quiz Answers And Chapter Review

A186

A187

Chapter 3

C205　　Chapter 4 Frequencies & Meaning

Chapter Quiz The Correct Answers Are Highlighted

1) Frequencies and combinations of Frequencies are the basis of what?

A) All Matter   B) All Circumstances

C) The Universe   **D) All**

A205 ↓

2) What is the basis of a Frequency?

A) Meaning That is Already Present   B) Meaning That You Assign

C) Either

A206

3) Frequencies can be added together to form:

A) More Complex Frequencies   B) Matter

C) The Universe   **D) All**

4) Frequencies Form What into Matter and Circumstances?

A) Energy   B) Stuff

C) Corn Starch   D) Rice

5) The essence of a Frequency is That it Causes Energy to:

A) Become Circumstance   B) Vibrate

C) Create Form   **D) All**

Quiz Answers And Chapter Review

Chapter 5 Resonance, The Secret
"Match-Making" Force Of The Universe   C285

Chapter Quiz The Correct Answers Are Highlighted

1) Resonance is a state when what occurs?

A) Like Frequencies Meet   B) Un-Like Frequencies Meet

C) Frequency Meets Energy   D) A Situation meets Matter

2) Resonance has the ability to do what?

A) Move huge masses   B) Elicit Responses From Like Frequencies

C) Bring into a mutual awareness people, situations and events

D) All

3) Resonance is a "Primary Force" second only to:

A) Electrical Force   B) Nuclear Force

C) Meanings & Their Frequencies   D) Gravity

4) Resonance has the power to:

A) Elicit a Specific Result from a Situation B) Create Mutual Awareness

C) Elicit Responses From Any Distance or Time   **D) All**

5) Resonance can be best described as:

A) The Universal Matchmaker B) Always Working & Always Effective

C) The "Enforcer" That Carries Out Your Meanings   **D) All**

Quiz Answers And Chapter Review

A285

A286

A287

4459695R00124

Made in the USA
San Bernardino, CA
23 September 2013